Contents:

Chapter 1: The Role of School

- The importance of strong leadership
- The skills and qualities of effective school leaders
- The challenges of school leadership
- How to overcome the challenges of school leadership

Chapter 2: Effective Communication – p36

- The different types of communication
- The importance of clear and concise communication
- How to build relationships through communication
- How to deal with difficult conversations

Chapter 3: Data-Driven Decision-Making – p43

- The importance of collecting data
- How to analyze data
- How to use data to make decisions
- How to avoid making decisions based on gut instinct

Chapter 4: Budgeting and Finance – p50

- The importance of a sound financial plan
- How to create a budget
- How to track expenses
- How to manage cash flow
- How to raise money

Chapter 5: Human Resources – p58

- The importance of hiring the right people
- How to develop and train employees
- How to create a positive work environment
- How to deal with employee performance issues

Chapter 6: Facilities Management – p64

- The importance of maintaining school facilities

- How to manage repairs and maintenance
- How to create a safe and secure environment
- How to comply with safety regulations

Chapter 7: Risk Management – p71

- The importance of identifying and managing risks
- How to develop a risk management plan
- How to respond to incidents
- How to mitigate future risks

Chapter 8: Compliance – p77

- The importance of complying with regulations
- How to identify and understand regulations
- How to develop a compliance plan
- How to monitor compliance

Conclusion – p83

Bibliography – p85

Acknowledgments

I would like to thank the following people for their help in making this book possible:

- My wife Stacey, for her love and support throughout this project.
- My children, Lillie and Sophie for their patience and understanding when I was working on the book.
- My parents, for their encouragement and inspiration.
- My friends, for their feedback and advice.

I would also like to thank all of the people who have shared their stories with me. Their experiences have helped me to understand the challenges and rewards of working in education, an invaluable asset to anyone.

Finally, I would like to thank you the reader for picking up this book. I hope you enjoy it.

Introduction to improving school management

- What is school leadership?

  School leadership is the process of guiding and overseeing a school's operations. It entails setting goals, developing strategies, and fostering a culture of learning and collaboration. School leaders play a critical role in the success of a school community. They are responsible for creating a safe and supportive environment, ensuring that all students have access to high-quality instruction, and developing a strong sense of community.

- Why is school leadership important?

  School leadership is important because it has a direct impact on student learning. Studies have shown that schools with strong leadership have higher student achievement rates. School leaders can also help to close the achievement gap and improve student outcomes for all students.

- How can school leadership be improved?

  There are a number of ways to improve school leadership. One way is to provide school leaders with professional development opportunities. This can help them develop the skills and knowledge they need to be effective leaders. Another way to improve school leadership is to foster a culture of collaboration and support. This can help school leaders share ideas and learn from each other. Finally, it is important to provide school leaders with the resources they need to be successful. This includes things like time, money, and access to data.

Chapter 1: The Role of School Leaders

> • "Leadership is about creating a vision, sharing it, and getting people excited about it." - Simon Sinek

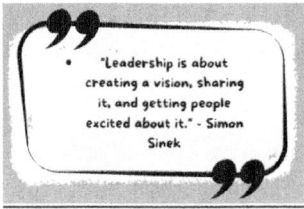

The first chapter of the book discusses the role of school leaders in improving administration. It covers topics such as:

- The importance of strong leadership
- The skills and qualities of effective school leaders
- The challenges of school leadership
- How to overcome the challenges of school leadership

The importance of strong leadership

Strong leadership is essential for the success of any school. Effective school leaders are able to create a positive learning environment, motivate and inspire teachers and students, and make sound decisions that are in the best interests of the school community.

Strong leadership in schools is essential for a number of reasons. First, it can help to create a positive and supportive learning environment. When students feel safe and supported, they are more likely to be engaged in their learning and to achieve their full potential. Second, strong leadership can help to ensure that all students have access to high-quality instruction. By setting high expectations for students and teachers, and by providing the resources and support needed to meet those expectations, strong leaders can help to close the achievement gap and ensure that all students have the opportunity to succeed. Third, strong leadership can help to build a strong school community. When teachers, students, parents, and other stakeholders work together towards a common goal, the school is more likely to be successful.

There are a number of qualities that are essential for strong school leaders. These include:

- Vision: Strong leaders have a clear vision for what they want their school to achieve. They are able to articulate this vision to others and to inspire them to work towards it.

- Communication: Strong leaders are effective communicators. They are able to communicate their vision clearly and concisely, and they are able to listen to and respond to the needs of others.

- Decision-making: Strong leaders are able to make sound decisions. They are able to gather information, weigh options, and make decisions that are in the best interests of their school community.

- Collaboration: Strong leaders are able to collaborate effectively with others. They are able to build relationships, work with others to achieve common goals, and resolve conflict.

- Resilience: Strong leaders are resilient. They are able to bounce back from setbacks and to maintain a positive attitude even in difficult times.

Strong leadership is essential for schools to be successful. By providing a positive learning environment, ensuring high-quality instruction, and building a strong school community, strong leaders can help all students to achieve their full potential.

Here are some additional benefits of strong leadership in schools:

- Increased student achievement
- Improved teacher morale
- Reduced teacher turnover
- Increased parental involvement
- Stronger school-community partnerships

- Improved school climate

If you are interested in becoming a strong school leader, there are a number of things you can do to develop the necessary skills and qualities. These include:

- Get involved in your school community. Volunteer to serve on committees, attend school events, and get to know your fellow students, teachers, and parents.

- Take leadership courses. There are many leadership courses available online and at local colleges and universities. These courses can help you to develop your leadership skills and to learn how to be an effective leader.

- Read books and articles about leadership. There are many great books and articles available that can teach you about leadership. Reading about the experiences of other leaders can help you to develop your own leadership style.

- Get feedback from others. Ask your friends, family, colleagues, and students for feedback on your leadership skills. This feedback can help you to identify areas where you can improve.

Becoming a strong school leader is a challenging but rewarding experience. By developing the necessary skills and qualities, you can make a positive difference in the lives of your students and in your school community.

Here are 10 of the top books on becoming a strong leader in schools:

1. The Principal's Compass: A School Leader's Guide to Achieving Excellence by Thomas J. Sergiovanni. This book provides a comprehensive guide to school leadership, covering topics such as vision, mission, culture, and decision-making.

2. Leadership for Learning: How Successful School Leaders Transform Teaching and Learning by Andy Hargreaves and Michael Fullan. This book focuses on the importance of leadership in creating a culture of learning in schools.

3. The Courage to Lead: Being a School Principal in an Age of Change by Linda Lambert. This book provides practical advice for school leaders on how to navigate the challenges of change.

4. The Smart Principal's Guide to Data-Driven Decision Making by Robert J. Marzano. This book provides a step-by-step guide to using data to improve student achievement.

5. Leading With Emotional Intelligence: A Practical Guide for School Leaders by Joseph Murphy and Erika Christakis. This book explores the importance of emotional intelligence for school leaders and provides strategies for developing this skill.

6. The Culture of Excellence: A School Leader's Guide to Building a High-Performing School by James P. Spillane. This book focuses on the importance of school culture and provides strategies for creating a culture of excellence.

7. Holding Fast to Our Values: How Good People Become Good Leaders by Michael Fullan. This book explores the importance of values-based leadership and provides strategies for leading with integrity.

8. The Turnaround: How Great Leaders Bring About Extraordinary Results by Paul Bambrick-Santoyo. This book provides a framework for leading school turnarounds.

9. The High-Trust School: How Trust Shapes School Culture and Instruction by Thomas W. Sergiovanni. This book explores the importance of trust in school leadership and provides strategies for building trust.

10. The School Leader's Guide to Thriving: A Practical Guide to Personal and Professional Well-Being by Todd Whitaker. This book provides practical advice for school leaders on how to take care of themselves physically, emotionally, and mentally.

There are many great books available on school leadership. By reading these books and reflecting on the ideas presented, you can develop the skills and qualities necessary to be an effective school leader.

The skills and qualities of effective school leaders

There are many different skills and qualities that effective school leaders possess. Some of the most important skills include:

Communication

- Effective school leaders are able to communicate effectively with teachers, students, parents, and other stakeholders. They are able to clearly articulate their vision for the school, build relationships, and resolve conflict.

  Communication is one of the most important skills for a school leader. Effective communication can help to build relationships, resolve conflict, and achieve common goals.

  Here are some tips for effective communication in schools:

- Be clear and concise. When communicating with others, be sure to be clear and concise. Avoid using jargon or technical terms that may not be understood by everyone.

- Be respectful. Always be respectful when communicating with others, even when you disagree with them.

- Be open to feedback. Be open to feedback from others. This will help you to improve your communication skills and to build relationships.

- Be a good listener. Listening is just as important as speaking. When someone is talking to you, give them your full attention and make eye contact.

- Be proactive. Don't wait for problems to arise before communicating with others. Be proactive and communicate regularly with your staff, students, and parents.

- Use a variety of communication channels. There are many different ways to communicate with others. In addition to face-to-face meetings, you can also use email, phone calls, letters, and newsletters.

  By following these tips, you can improve your communication skills and become a more effective school leader.

  Here are some specific examples of how effective communication can be used in schools:

- A school leader can use communication to build relationships with teachers, students, and parents. By communicating regularly with these stakeholders, the school leader can get to know them better and build trust. This trust can then be used to support the school's goals and objectives.

- A school leader can use communication to resolve conflict. When conflict arises, the school leader can use communication to help the parties involved understand each other's perspectives and to find a mutually agreeable solution.

- A school leader can use communication to achieve common goals. By communicating the school's goals and objectives to all stakeholders, the school leader can get everyone on the same page and working towards the same thing. This can lead to improved student achievement and a more successful school.

Communication is a critical skill for school leaders. By using communication effectively, school leaders can build relationships, resolve conflict, and achieve common goals.

Vision:

Effective school leaders have a clear vision for the future of their school. They are able to articulate this vision to others and inspire them to work towards it. A clear vision provides a sense of direction and purpose for the school community. It can help to motivate and unite staff, students, and parents behind a common goal.

Here are some tips for developing a clear vision for your school:

- Start by reflecting on your values and beliefs about education. What do you believe is important for students to learn? What kind of learning environment do you want to create?

- Consider the needs of your students and community. What are the challenges and opportunities facing your school? What do your students need to succeed?

- Do some research on successful schools. What are the characteristics of these schools? What are they doing that is different?

- Brainstorm with your staff, students, and parents. Get their input on what they want for the school.

- Once you have a general idea of your vision, start to develop a more specific plan. What are the goals you want to achieve? What are the steps you need to take to achieve those goals?

- Communicate your vision to your school community. Share your vision with staff, students, and parents. Get them excited about the future of your school.

- Celebrate your successes along the way. When you achieve a goal, take the time to celebrate with your school community. This will help to keep everyone motivated and moving forward.

By following these tips, you can develop a clear vision for your school that can inspire and motivate everyone involved.

Here are some specific examples of how a clear vision can benefit a school:

- A clear vision can help to improve student achievement. When everyone in the school community is working towards the same goal, it can lead to improved student outcomes.

- A clear vision can help to create a more positive school climate. When students, staff, and parents are all working towards the same goal, it can create a more positive and supportive school environment.

- A clear vision can help to attract and retain top talent. When potential employees know that the school has a clear vision and is committed to achieving that vision, they are more likely to want to work there.

A clear vision is essential for any school that wants to be successful. By developing a clear vision and communicating it to your school community, you can inspire and motivate everyone involved and help your school achieve its goals.

Decision-making

This is a critical skill for school leaders. Effective school leaders are able to make sound decisions that are in the best interests of the school community. They are able to gather information, weigh the pros and cons of different options, and make a decision that is based on evidence.

Here are some tips for making sound decisions as a school leader:

- Gather information. Before making a decision, it is important to gather as much information as possible. This information can come from a variety of sources, including staff, students, parents, experts, and data.

- Weigh the pros and cons. Once you have gathered information, it is important to weigh the pros and cons of different options. This will help you to identify the option that is most likely to achieve your desired outcome.

- Make a decision. After weighing the pros and cons, it is time to make a decision. When making a decision, it is important to be confident in your decision and to be prepared to defend it.

- Be flexible. Even the best-made decisions can sometimes need to be changed. It is important to be flexible and to be willing to change your decision if new information becomes available.

- Communicate your decision. Once you have made a decision, it is important to communicate it to your school community. This will help to ensure that everyone is on the same page and that everyone is working towards the same goal.

By following these tips, you can make sound decisions that are in the best interests of your school community.

Here are some specific examples of how effective decision-making can benefit a school:

- Effective decision-making can help to improve student achievement. When school leaders make decisions that are based on evidence, it can lead to improved student outcomes.

- Effective decision-making can help to create a more positive school climate. When school leaders make decisions that are fair and equitable, it can create a more positive and supportive school environment.

- Effective decision-making can help to attract and retain top talent. When potential employees know that the school has a strong decision-making process, they are more likely to want to work there.

Decision-making is an essential skill for any school leader. By developing the ability to make sound decisions, school leaders can help their schools achieve their goals.

Problem-solving

Problem-solving is a critical skill for school leaders. Effective school leaders are able to identify and solve problems that arise in the school environment. They are able to think creatively and come up with solutions that are both effective and sustainable.

Here are some tips for problem-solving as a school leader:

- Identify the problem. The first step in solving a problem is to identify the problem. What is the specific issue that needs to be addressed?

- Gather information. Once you have identified the problem, it is important to gather information. This information can come from a variety of sources, including staff, students, parents, experts, and data.

- Brainstorm solutions. Once you have gathered information, it is time to brainstorm solutions. This is where you can start to think creatively and come up with a variety of possible solutions.

- Evaluate solutions. Once you have brainstormed a variety of solutions, it is time to evaluate them. This means considering the pros and cons of each solution and identifying the solution that is most likely to be effective.

- Implement the solution. Once you have selected a solution, it is time to implement it. This means putting the solution into action and monitoring its progress.

- Evaluate the solution. After implementing the solution, it is important to evaluate it. This means assessing whether the solution was effective and identifying any areas where it can be improved.

By following these tips, you can solve problems that arise in the school environment.

Here are some specific examples of how effective problem-solving can benefit a school:

- Effective problem-solving can help to improve student achievement. When school leaders solve problems that are affecting student learning, it can lead to improved student outcomes.

- Effective problem-solving can help to create a more positive school climate. When school leaders solve problems that are causing conflict or tension, it can create a more positive and supportive school environment.

- Effective problem-solving can help to attract and retain top talent. When potential employees know that the school has a strong problem-solving process, they are more likely to want to work there.

Problem-solving is an essential skill for any school leader. By developing the ability to solve problems, school leaders can help their schools achieve their goals.

Here are some additional tips for effective problem-solving:

- Be open to new ideas. Don't be afraid to consider new and innovative solutions to problems.

- Be willing to take risks. Sometimes, the best solutions are the ones that involve taking risks.

- Be persistent. Don't give up on a problem until you have found a solution that works.

- Be positive. A positive attitude can go a long way in solving problems.

By following these tips, you can become a more effective problem-solver and help your school achieve its goals.

Collaboration

Collaboration is a critical skill for school leaders. Effective school leaders are able to collaborate with others to achieve common goals. They are able to build relationships with teachers, students, parents, and other stakeholders and work together to create a positive learning environment.

Here are some tips for collaborating as a school leader:

- Build relationships. The first step in collaborating is to build relationships with others. This means getting to know them, understanding their strengths and weaknesses, and building trust.

- Be open to feedback. Once you have built relationships, it is important to be open to feedback. This means being willing to listen to others and to consider their ideas.

- Be willing to compromise. Collaboration often involves compromise. This means being willing to give up something in order to reach a common goal.

- Be a good listener. Listening is just as important as speaking. When someone is talking to you, give them your full attention and make eye contact.

- Be respectful. Always be respectful when collaborating with others, even when you disagree with them.

- Be positive. A positive attitude can go a long way in collaboration.

By following these tips, you can become a more effective collaborator and help your school achieve its goals.

Here are some specific examples of how collaboration can benefit a school:

- Collaboration can help to improve student achievement. When teachers, students, and parents collaborate, it can lead to improved student outcomes.

- Collaboration can help to create a more positive school climate. When everyone in the school community feels like they are part of a team, it can create a more positive and supportive school environment.

- Collaboration can help to attract and retain top talent. When potential employees know that the school has a strong collaborative culture, they are more likely to want to work there.

Collaboration is an essential skill for any school leader. By developing the ability to collaborate, school leaders can help their schools achieve their goals.

Here are some additional tips for effective collaboration:

- Set clear goals. Before you start collaborating, it is important to set clear goals. What do you want to achieve by collaborating?

- Create a plan. Once you have set clear goals, it is time to create a plan. This plan should include the steps you need to take to achieve your goals.

- Communicate regularly. It is important to communicate regularly with your collaborators. This will help to ensure that everyone is on the same page and that everyone is working towards the same goal.

- Celebrate successes. When you achieve a goal, take the time to celebrate with your collaborators. This will help to keep everyone motivated and moving forward.

By following these tips, you can collaborate effectively and help your school achieve its goals.

Trust:

Trust is a critical component of effective school leadership. Trust is built when school leaders are honest, transparent, and fair in their dealings with others. They are also willing to listen to others and take their feedback into account.

Here are some specific examples of how trust can benefit a school:

- Trust can help to improve student achievement. When students trust their teachers and administrators, they are more likely to be engaged in learning and to achieve their academic goals.

- Trust can help to create a more positive school climate. When staff, students, and parents trust each other, it can create a more positive and supportive school environment.

- Trust can help to attract and retain top talent. When potential employees know that they can trust their colleagues and supervisors, they are more likely to want to work at the school.

Trust is an essential ingredient for any successful school. By building trust with others, school leaders can create a positive and supportive environment where students, staff, and parents can thrive.

Here are some tips for building trust as a school leader:

- Be honest and transparent. Always be honest with others, even when it is difficult. Be transparent about your decision-making process and the reasons behind your decisions.

- Be fair. Treat everyone fairly, regardless of their position or background.

- Be willing to listen. Take the time to listen to others and to understand their perspectives.

- Be open to feedback. Be willing to receive feedback from others and to use that feedback to improve your leadership.

- Be consistent. Be consistent in your actions and your words. This will help others to trust that you are reliable and trustworthy.

By following these tips, you can build trust with others and create a positive and supportive environment where students, staff, and parents can thrive.

Here are some additional tips for building trust:

- Be mindful of your body language. Your body language can communicate a lot about your trustworthiness. Make eye contact, smile, and nod your head to show that you are listening and engaged.

- Be mindful of your tone of voice. Your tone of voice can also communicate a lot about your trustworthiness. Speak calmly and confidently.

- Be mindful of your words. Choose your words carefully. Avoid using sarcasm or hurtful language.

By being mindful of your body language, tone of voice, and words, you can build trust with others and create a positive and supportive environment where students, staff, and parents can thrive.

The challenges of school leadership

School leaders face a number of challenges, including:

Increasing demands on schools

Schools are under increasing pressure to improve student achievement, provide a safe and supportive learning environment, and meet the needs of a diverse student population. These demands are putting a strain on schools and making it difficult for them to meet all of their goals.

Here are some of the factors that are contributing to the increasing demands on schools:

- The rising cost of education. The cost of education is rising, which is putting a strain on school budgets. This makes it difficult for schools to hire qualified teachers, provide adequate resources, and maintain safe and up-to-date facilities.

- The growing diversity of the student population. The student population in the United States is becoming increasingly diverse, which is presenting new challenges for schools. Schools need to find ways to meet the needs of students from different backgrounds and with different learning styles.

- The increasing focus on standardized testing. There is a growing focus on standardized testing in schools, which is putting pressure on teachers to teach to the test. This can lead to a narrowing of the curriculum and a focus on rote learning rather than critical thinking.

- The increasing expectations of parents. Parents have high expectations for their children's education, which is putting pressure on schools to perform at a high level. Parents want their children to be prepared for college and for the workforce, and they are looking to schools to provide the necessary skills and knowledge.

The increasing demands on schools are making it difficult for them to meet all of their goals. Schools are struggling to improve student achievement, provide a safe and supportive learning environment, and meet the needs of a diverse student population. These challenges are likely to continue in the future, and schools will need to find new ways to meet the needs of their students.

Here are some of the strategies that schools can use to address the increasing demands on them:

- Work with parents and community members to develop a shared vision for education. This will help to ensure that everyone is working towards the same goals.

- Invest in professional development for teachers. This will help teachers to stay up-to-date on the latest teaching methods and to learn how to meet the needs of all students.

- Use data to inform decision-making. This will help schools to identify areas where they need to improve and to allocate resources accordingly.

- Create a culture of collaboration. This will help schools to pool their resources and expertise to address the challenges they face.

- Be flexible and adaptable. The demands on schools are constantly changing, so schools need to be able to adapt to meet those changes.

By using these strategies, schools can address the increasing demands on them and continue to provide a high-quality education for all students.

Limited resources

Schools often have limited resources, which can make it difficult to provide the best possible education for students. Here are some of the challenges that schools face when they have limited resources:

- Acquiring and maintaining materials: Schools may struggle to acquire and maintain the necessary materials, such as textbooks, computers, and other equipment. This can make it difficult for teachers to provide a high-quality education.

- Providing enrichment opportunities: Schools may not have the resources to provide enrichment opportunities, such as extracurricular activities, field trips, and after-school programs. This can limit students' opportunities to learn and grow outside of the classroom.

- Attracting and retaining qualified teachers: Schools may have difficulty attracting and retaining qualified teachers, due to low salaries and lack of resources. This can lead to a shortage of qualified teachers, which can impact the quality of education that students receive.

- Meeting the needs of all students: Schools may struggle to meet the needs of all students, such as students with special needs, English language learners, and students from low-income families. This can lead to disparities in educational outcomes.

Despite these challenges, there are a number of things that schools can do to overcome the limitations of limited resources. Here are some strategies that schools can use:

- Partner with community organizations: Schools can partner with community organizations to provide resources and support that they may not be able to afford on their own. For example, a community organization may be able to donate computers or provide space for after-school programs.

- Use technology: Technology can be a valuable resource for schools, as it can be used to provide enrichment opportunities, deliver instruction, and communicate with parents. Schools can use technology to supplement their limited resources and provide a high-quality education for students.

- Get creative: Schools can get creative in finding ways to provide a high-quality education with limited resources. For example, teachers can use recycled materials to create learning materials, or students can participate in service learning projects to gain real-world experience.

- Focus on the basics: Schools can focus on providing students with the basic skills they need to succeed, such as reading, writing, and math. This will help students to be successful, even if they do not have access to all of the resources they need.

By using these strategies, schools can overcome the limitations of limited resources and provide a high-quality education for all students.

Changing demographics

The demographics of the student population are changing, which can pose challenges for schools. For example, schools are seeing an increase in the number of students from low-income families and students with special needs.

Here are some of the challenges that schools face when the demographics of the student population change:

- Language barriers: Schools may have students who do not speak English as a first language. This can create challenges for teachers who are not fluent in the students' native language.

- Cultural differences: Schools may have students from different cultures. This can create challenges for teachers who are not familiar with the students' culture.

- Special needs: Schools may have students with special needs, such as learning disabilities or physical disabilities. This can create challenges for teachers who are not trained to work with students with special needs.

- Low-income families: Schools may have students from low-income families. This can create challenges for schools, as they may not have the resources to provide the support that these students need.

Despite these challenges, there are a number of things that schools can do to meet the needs of a changing student population. Here are some strategies that schools can use:

- Provide professional development for teachers: Schools can provide professional development for teachers on how to work with students from different cultures, languages, and special needs.
- Create a welcoming environment: Schools can create a welcoming environment for all students, regardless of their background. This can be done by displaying posters and artwork that reflect the diversity of the student population.
- Provide support services: Schools can provide support services for students who need them, such as tutoring, counseling, and after-school programs.
- Partner with community organizations: Schools can partner with community organizations to provide resources and support that they may not be able to afford on their own. For example, a community organization may be able to provide tutors or mentors for students.

By using these strategies, schools can meet the needs of a changing student population and provide all students with the opportunity to succeed.

Here are some additional tips for schools:

- Be flexible: The needs of students and families may change over time, so schools need to be flexible and adaptable.
- Be inclusive: Schools should be welcoming to all students, regardless of their background.
- Be supportive: Schools should provide support to all students, so they can reach their full potential.

By following these tips, schools can create a positive learning environment for all students.

External pressures

Schools are often subject to external pressures from parents, politicians, and the media. These pressures can make it difficult for school leaders to make decisions that are in the best interests of the school community.

Here are some of the external pressures that schools face:

- Parental pressure: Parents may pressure schools to make decisions that align with their own personal beliefs or values. For example, parents may pressure schools to teach creationism instead of evolution, or to teach abstinence-only sex education instead of comprehensive sex education.

- Political pressure: Politicians may pressure schools to make decisions that align with their own political agenda. For example, politicians may pressure schools to cut funding for arts programs or to reduce the number of elective courses that are offered.

- Media pressure: The media can also put pressure on schools. For example, the media may criticize schools for their handling of a particular incident, or they may report on a school's test scores in a negative light.

These external pressures can make it difficult for school leaders to make decisions that are in the best interests of the school community. School leaders need to be able to balance the needs of all stakeholders, including parents, politicians, the media, and the students themselves.

Here are some tips for school leaders who are facing external pressures:

- Communicate with all stakeholders: School leaders need to communicate with all stakeholders, including parents, politicians, the media, and the students themselves. This will help to ensure that everyone is aware of the school's decisions and why they were made.

- Be transparent: School leaders need to be transparent about their decision-making process. This will help to build trust with stakeholders and make it more likely that they will support the school's decisions.

- Be willing to compromise: School leaders need to be willing to compromise. This is often necessary in order to reach a decision that is acceptable to all stakeholders.

- Be firm: School leaders need to be firm in their decision-making. This is important in order to avoid being bullied by stakeholders who may have different agendas.

By following these tips, school leaders can manage external pressures and make decisions that are in the best interests of the school community.

Here are some additional tips for schools:

- Create a culture of trust and transparency: Schools should create a culture of trust and transparency, where all stakeholders feel comfortable sharing their views and concerns. This will help to build trust and make it more likely that stakeholders will support the school's decisions.

- Have a strong communication plan: Schools should have a strong communication plan in place, so that they can effectively communicate with all stakeholders. This plan should include a variety of communication channels, such as email, social media, and newsletters.

- Be proactive: Schools should be proactive in communicating with stakeholders. This means reaching out to stakeholders regularly, rather than waiting for them to come to the school with concerns.

- Be responsive: Schools should be responsive to stakeholder feedback. This means listening to stakeholder concerns and taking steps to address them.

By following these tips, schools can manage external pressures and build strong relationships with stakeholders.

How to overcome the challenges of school leadership

There are a number of ways that school leaders can overcome the challenges they face. Some of the most effective strategies include:

Building a strong team

Building a strong team is essential for any school leader. A strong team can help to achieve the school's mission and goals. Here are some tips for building a strong team:

1. Hire the right people. When hiring new teachers, administrators, and support staff, it is important to look for people who are committed to the school's mission and goals. These are people who are passionate about education and who want to make a difference in the lives of students.

2. Create a positive work environment. A positive work environment is one where everyone feels valued and respected. It is important to create a culture of collaboration and teamwork, where everyone feels comfortable sharing ideas and working together to achieve common goals.

3. Provide professional development opportunities. Professional development is essential for keeping staff up-to-date on the latest teaching methods and best practices. It is also a great way to build relationships and create a sense of community among staff.

4. Celebrate successes. It is important to celebrate successes, both big and small. This will help to boost morale and keep staff motivated.

5. Provide feedback. Feedback is essential for professional growth. It is important to provide staff with regular feedback, both positive and constructive. This will help them to improve their skills and knowledge.

6. Be supportive. School leaders need to be supportive of their staff. This means providing them with the resources they need to be successful, and it also means being there to offer guidance and support when needed.

By following these tips, school leaders can build a strong team that is committed to the school's mission and goals.

Here are some additional tips for building a strong team:

- Be clear about the school's mission and goals. Make sure that everyone on the team understands the school's mission and goals. This will help them to stay focused and motivated.

- Set clear expectations. Let everyone on the team know what is expected of them. This will help them to perform at their best.

- Provide opportunities for growth. Encourage staff to take on new challenges and to develop their skills. This will help them to grow professionally and make a greater contribution to the school.

- Recognize and reward achievement. When staff members do a good job, be sure to recognize and reward their achievement. This will help to motivate them to continue to do their best.

By following these tips, school leaders can build a strong team that is committed to the school's mission and goals.

Communicating effectively

Communicating effectively is essential for any school leader. Effective communication can help to build trust, resolve conflicts, and achieve the school's mission and goals. Here are some tips for communicating effectively with all stakeholders:

1. Be clear and concise. When communicating with stakeholders, it is important to be clear and concise. Avoid using jargon or technical terms that may not be understood by everyone.

2. Be honest and transparent. Stakeholders need to be able to trust that the information they are receiving is accurate and truthful. Be honest about the challenges facing the school and the steps being taken to address them.

3. Be open to feedback. Stakeholders should feel comfortable sharing their feedback with the school leadership. Be open to hearing what they have to say and be willing to make changes based on their feedback.

4. Be proactive. Don't wait for stakeholders to come to you with concerns. Be proactive in communicating with them and in addressing their concerns.

5. Use a variety of communication channels. Not everyone prefers to communicate in the same way. Use a variety of communication channels, such as email, social media, and newsletters, to reach out to stakeholders.

6. Be responsive. When stakeholders reach out to you, be sure to respond promptly. This shows that you value their time and that you are taking their concerns seriously.

By following these tips, school leaders can communicate effectively with all stakeholders and build strong relationships.

Here are some additional tips for communicating effectively:

- Be aware of your audience. Tailor your communication to the specific audience you are trying to reach. For example, you may use different language and tone when communicating with parents than you would when communicating with students.

- Use visuals. Visuals can be a great way to communicate complex information in a clear and concise way. For example, you could use infographics or charts to illustrate your points.

- Be patient. It may take time to build trust and rapport with stakeholders. Be patient and persistent in your communication efforts.

By following these tips, school leaders can communicate effectively with all stakeholders and build strong relationships.

Developing a positive school culture

A positive school culture is one where students feel safe, supported, and motivated to learn. It is a place where students feel like they belong and where they can thrive. Here are some tips for developing a positive school culture:

1. Set clear expectations. Let students know what is expected of them in terms of behaviour, academics, and participation. This will help them to understand what is required of them and to meet those expectations.

2. Be consistent. Be consistent in your expectations and in your enforcement of those expectations. This will help students to understand that you are serious about creating a positive school culture.

3. Be fair. Be fair in your treatment of all students. This will help to build trust and respect among students and staff.

4. Be supportive. Be supportive of students' academic, social, and emotional needs. This will help students to feel safe and supported, and it will motivate them to learn.

5. Celebrate successes. Celebrate students' successes, both big and small. This will help to boost morale and keep students motivated.

6. Be positive. Be positive in your interactions with students and staff. This will help to create a positive and productive environment.

7. Be a role model. Be a role model for students and staff by demonstrating the behaviours that you want to see in others. This will help to create a culture of respect and responsibility.

By following these tips, school leaders can create a positive school culture where students feel safe, supported, and motivated to learn.

Here are some additional tips for developing a positive school culture:

- Involve students in the process. Ask students for their input on how to create a positive school culture. This will help them to feel like they are part of the solution and that their voices are being heard.

- Create opportunities for collaboration. Provide opportunities for students to collaborate with each other on projects and activities. This will help them to learn from each other and to develop positive relationships.

- Encourage creativity and innovation. Encourage students to be creative and to think outside the box. This will help them to develop their problem-solving skills and to be more engaged in their learning.

- Promote diversity and inclusion. Promote diversity and inclusion in the school community. This will help students to learn about different cultures and perspectives, and it will help them to develop a more open-minded and tolerant worldview.

By following these tips, school leaders can create a positive school culture that is beneficial for all students.

Focusing on student achievement

Student achievement is the ultimate goal of all schools. School leaders need to focus on improving student achievement by providing high-quality instruction, providing support for struggling students, and holding students accountable for their learning.

Here are some specific strategies that school leaders can use to focus on student achievement:

1. Provide high-quality instruction: High-quality instruction is essential for improving student achievement. School leaders can ensure that high-quality instruction is taking place by hiring qualified teachers, providing teachers with professional development, and creating a culture of continuous improvement.

2. Provide support for struggling students: Not all students learn at the same pace. Some students may need additional support to succeed. School leaders can provide support for struggling students by providing tutoring, after-school programs, and other resources.

3. Hold students accountable for their learning: Students need to be held accountable for their learning in order to improve. School leaders can hold

students accountable for their learning by setting clear expectations, providing regular feedback, and using assessments to track student progress.

By following these strategies, school leaders can focus on improving student achievement and ensuring that all students have the opportunity to succeed.

Here are some additional tips for focusing on student achievement:

- Set clear goals: School leaders need to set clear goals for student achievement. These goals should be measurable, achievable, relevant, and time-bound.

- Track progress: School leaders need to track progress towards their goals. This will help them to identify areas where improvement is needed and to make adjustments to their plans.

- Communicate with stakeholders: School leaders need to communicate with stakeholders about their goals and progress. This will help to build support for their efforts and to ensure that everyone is working towards the same objectives.

- Celebrate successes: School leaders need to celebrate successes, both big and small. This will help to boost morale and keep everyone motivated.

By following these tips, school leaders can focus on improving student achievement and ensuring that all students have the opportunity to succeed.

Using data to make decisions

Data is essential for making informed decisions about instruction, curriculum, and school improvement. By collecting and analyzing data, school leaders can identify areas where students are struggling and make changes to improve instruction and curriculum.

Here are some specific ways that school leaders can use data to make decisions:

1. Identify areas where students are struggling: By looking at data on student achievement, school leaders can identify areas where students are struggling.

This information can be used to target instruction and interventions to help students succeed.

2. Make decisions about instruction: Data can be used to make decisions about instruction, such as what materials to use, what methods to employ, and how to group students. For example, if data shows that students are struggling with a particular concept, the school leader may decide to provide additional instruction on that concept.

3. Make decisions about curriculum: Data can also be used to make decisions about curriculum, such as what topics to cover, how much time to spend on each topic, and what assessments to use. For example, if data shows that students are not mastering a particular topic, the school leader may decide to add more time for instruction on that topic.

4. Make decisions about school improvement: Data can also be used to make decisions about school improvement, such as how to allocate resources, what professional development to offer teachers, and how to measure progress. For example, if data shows that students are not making adequate progress, the school leader may decide to reallocate resources to provide more support for struggling students.

By using data to make decisions, school leaders can ensure that all students have the opportunity to succeed.

Here are some additional tips for using data to make decisions:

- Collect data from multiple sources: Data can be collected from a variety of sources, such as standardized tests, teacher-made assessments, and attendance records. By collecting data from multiple sources, school leaders can get a more complete picture of student achievement.

- Analyze data carefully: Once data has been collected, it is important to analyze it carefully. This involves looking for trends, patterns, and outliers. By carefully analyzing data, school leaders can identify areas where students are struggling and make changes to improve instruction and curriculum.

- Communicate data findings with stakeholders: Once data has been analyzed, it is important to communicate the findings with stakeholders. This includes parents, teachers, administrators, and community members. By communicating data findings, school leaders can build support for their efforts and ensure that everyone is working towards the same objectives.

By following these tips, school leaders can use data to make informed decisions that will improve student achievement.

<u>Being flexible and adaptable</u>

The world is constantly changing, and so are the needs of students and the community. School leaders need to be flexible and adaptable in order to respond to these changes.

Here are some specific ways that school leaders can be flexible and adaptable:

1. Be open to new ideas: School leaders need to be open to new ideas and approaches to education. This means being willing to listen to the ideas of others, even if they are different from your own.
2. Be willing to change: School leaders need to be willing to change their practices and policies in order to meet the needs of students and the community. This may require making difficult decisions, but it is essential for ensuring that all students have the opportunity to succeed.
3. Be creative: School leaders need to be creative in order to find solutions to problems and challenges. This means thinking outside the box and coming up with new and innovative ideas.
4. Be collaborative: School leaders need to be collaborative in order to work effectively with others. This means building relationships with teachers, staff, parents, and community members.
5. Be positive: School leaders need to be positive in order to create a positive and productive environment. This means being optimistic and having a can-do attitude.

By being flexible and adaptable, school leaders can ensure that their schools are responsive to the changing needs of students and the community.

Here are some additional tips for being flexible and adaptable:

- Be willing to take risks: School leaders need to be willing to take risks in order to try new things. This may mean taking on new challenges or investing in new programs.

- Be willing to fail: School leaders need to be willing to fail in order to learn and grow. This means not being afraid to make mistakes and not being afraid to admit when you are wrong.

- Be persistent: School leaders need to be persistent in order to achieve their goals. This means not giving up when things get tough and not giving up on students who are struggling.

By following these tips, school leaders can be flexible and adaptable in order to meet the needs of students and the community.

Developing the skills and qualities

Here is a detailed analysis on developing the skills and qualities of an effective school leader and by overcoming the challenges they face, school leaders can make a positive difference in the lives of students and the community:

School leaders play a vital role in the lives of students and the community. They are responsible for creating a positive learning environment, providing high-quality instruction, and ensuring that all students have the opportunity to succeed.

There are many challenges that school leaders face, but by developing the skills and qualities of an effective leader, they can overcome these challenges and make a positive difference.

Here are some of the skills and qualities of an effective school leader:

1. Vision: Effective school leaders have a clear vision for their school. They know what they want their school to achieve, and they are able to articulate this vision to others.

2. Communication: Effective school leaders are able to communicate effectively with a variety of stakeholders, including teachers, students, parents, and community members. They are able to listen to others, build relationships, and share information in a clear and concise way.

3. Collaboration: Effective school leaders are able to collaborate effectively with others. They are able to build teams, delegate tasks, and work towards common goals.

4. Decision-making: Effective school leaders are able to make sound decisions. They are able to gather information, weigh options, and make decisions that are in the best interests of their students and their school.

5. Problem-solving: Effective school leaders are able to solve problems. They are able to identify problems, generate solutions, and implement solutions that are effective.

6. Resilience: Effective school leaders are resilient. They are able to bounce back from setbacks and continue to work towards their goals.

By developing these skills and qualities, school leaders can overcome the challenges they face and make a positive difference in the lives of students and the community.

Here are some specific examples of how school leaders can make a positive difference:

- They can create a positive learning environment where students feel safe, supported, and motivated to learn.
- They can provide high-quality instruction that meets the needs of all students.
- They can ensure that all students have access to resources and opportunities that will help them succeed.

- They can build relationships with students, teachers, parents, and community members.

- They can advocate for students and their needs.

- They can make decisions that are in the best interests of their students.

- They can solve problems that arise in the school.

- They can create a culture of continuous improvement where everyone is working to make the school better.

By doing these things, school leaders can make a positive difference in the lives of students and the community. They can help students succeed academically, socially, and emotionally. They can help create a better future for their community.

If you are interested in becoming a school leader, there are many resources available to help you. You can talk to your school principal, attend workshops and conferences, or read books and articles about school leadership. With hard work and dedication, you can develop the skills and qualities necessary to make a positive difference in the lives of students and the community.

Chapter 2: Effective Communication

> • "The single biggest problem in communication is the illusion that it has taken place." - George Bernard Shaw

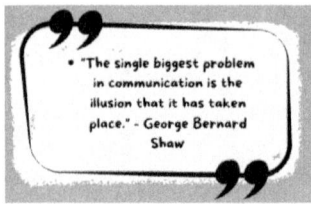

The second chapter of the book discusses the importance of effective communication in school administration. It covers topics such as:

- The different types of communication
- The importance of clear and concise communication
- How to build relationships through communication
- How to deal with difficult conversations

The different types of communication

Effective communication is essential for school administrators. It is the foundation of building relationships, resolving conflicts, and achieving goals. There are many different types of communication, including verbal, nonverbal, and written. Each type has its own strengths and weaknesses, and school administrators should use a variety of communication methods to reach their audience.

Verbal communication is the most common type of communication in schools. It includes face-to-face conversations, phone calls, and meetings. Verbal communication is often the most effective way to build relationships and resolve conflicts. However, it can be difficult to convey complex information or ideas verbally.

Nonverbal communication includes body language, facial expressions, and tone of voice. Nonverbal communication can be just as important as verbal communication, and it can often convey more meaning. For example, a smile can convey happiness or a frown can convey sadness. School administrators should be aware of their own nonverbal communication, and they should also pay attention to the nonverbal communication of others.

Written communication includes emails, letters, reports, and presentations. Written communication is often used to communicate information to a large audience or to document decisions. Written communication can be more effective than verbal communication for conveying complex information or ideas. However, it can be more difficult to build relationships and resolve conflicts through written communication.

School administrators should use a variety of communication methods to reach their audience. They should also be aware of the strengths and weaknesses of each type of communication. By using effective communication, school administrators can build relationships, resolve conflicts, and achieve goals.

Here are some tips for effective communication in school administration:

- Be clear and concise. When communicating, be sure to get your point across in a clear and concise way. Avoid using jargon or technical terms that your audience may not understand.

- Be respectful. Always be respectful of your audience, even if you disagree with them. Avoid using sarcasm or insults.

- Be open to feedback. Be willing to listen to feedback from your audience. This will help you to improve your communication skills.

- Be patient. It may take time to build trust and rapport with your audience. Be patient and persistent in your communication efforts.

The importance of clear and concise communication

Clear and concise communication is essential for successful education. It is important for teachers, students, and parents to be able to communicate effectively with each other. This allows for the smooth running of the school, as well as the best possible learning outcomes for students.

There are many benefits to clear and concise communication in education. For example, it:

- Improves understanding: When information is communicated clearly and concisely, it is easier for people to understand. This can lead to better learning outcomes for students, as they will be able to understand the material that is being taught.

- Reduces misunderstandings: When communication is clear and concise, it is less likely that there will be misunderstandings. This can help to prevent conflict and ensure that everyone is on the same page.

- Builds trust: When people feel that they are being communicated with clearly and concisely, they are more likely to trust the person who is communicating with them. This can lead to better relationships between teachers, students, and parents.

- Creates a positive learning environment: When communication is clear and concise, it creates a positive learning environment. This is because students feel that they are being respected and that their needs are being met.

There are many things that can be done to improve clear and concise communication in education. For example, teachers can:

- Use plain language: Avoid using jargon or technical terms that students may not understand.

- Be specific: When giving instructions, be as specific as possible.

- Use visuals: Visuals can help to illustrate concepts and make them easier to understand.

- Be patient: It may take time for students to understand complex concepts. Be patient and be willing to repeat yourself if necessary.

Students can also improve their communication skills by:

- Paying attention: When teachers are giving instructions, pay attention and make sure that you understand what is being said.

- Asking questions: If you do not understand something, do not be afraid to ask questions.

- Taking notes: Taking notes can help you to remember information and to understand concepts better.

- Practicing: The more you practice communicating, the better you will become at it.

  Parents can also play a role in improving clear and concise communication in education by:

- Communicating with teachers: Make an effort to communicate with your child's teachers on a regular basis. This will help you to stay informed about your child's progress and to ensure that there are no misunderstandings.

- Supporting your child's learning: Help your child to learn at home by providing them with resources and by encouraging them to practice.

- Encouraging good communication skills: Encourage your child to communicate clearly and concisely. This will help them to succeed in school and in life.

How to build relationships through communication

Communication is key to building relationships in education. It allows teachers, students, and parents to get to know each other better, share ideas, and build trust. There are many ways to communicate effectively in education, including:

- Face-to-face conversations: Face-to-face conversations are the most effective way to build relationships. They allow for two-way communication and for building rapport.

- Email: Email is a convenient way to communicate with people who are not physically present. It can be used to share information, ask questions, and provide feedback.

- Phone calls: Phone calls can be used to have quick conversations or to discuss more complex topics. They can also be used to follow up on emails or to schedule meetings.

- Letters: Letters can be used to communicate with people who are not easily accessible by phone or email. They can be used to share personal information or to express gratitude.

- Social media: Social media can be used to connect with people who are not part of the traditional school community. It can be used to share information, ask questions, and provide feedback.

Here are some tips for building relationships through communication in education:

- Be open and honest: When communicating, be open and honest about your thoughts and feelings. This will help to build trust and rapport.
- Be respectful: Always be respectful of the person you are communicating with, even if you disagree with them.
- Be patient: It may take time to build relationships through communication. Be patient and persistent in your efforts.
- Be positive: A positive attitude can go a long way in building relationships. Be positive and encouraging in your communications.

By following these tips, you can build strong relationships through communication in education. These relationships will help to create a positive learning environment for all.

Here are some additional tips for building relationships through communication in education:

- Get to know your students: Take the time to get to know your students on a personal level. Learn about their interests, their families, and their goals.
- Be approachable: Make yourself available to your students and let them know that you are there to help them.
- Be supportive: Offer your support to your students both academically and emotionally.
- Be fair: Be fair in your dealings with your students. Treat them all with respect, regardless of their academic abilities or their background.
- Be consistent: Be consistent in your expectations and your behavior. This will help your students feel safe and secure.

How to deal with difficult conversations

Difficult conversations are a normal part of life, but they can be especially challenging in the education setting. Here are some tips for dealing with difficult conversations in education:

1. Be prepared. Before you have the conversation, take some time to think about what you want to say and how you want to say it. This will help you stay calm and focused during the conversation.

2. Listen actively. When the other person is talking, listen carefully and try to understand their point of view. This will help you build trust and rapport, and it will also help you to come up with a solution that is agreeable to both parties.

3. Be respectful. Even if you disagree with the other person, it is important to be respectful of their feelings and their opinions. This will help to keep the conversation from becoming heated and unproductive.

4. Be open to compromise. It is rare that one person will get everything they want in a difficult conversation. Be willing to compromise and find a solution that works for everyone involved.

5. Follow up. After the conversation, send a follow-up email or letter to reiterate the key points that were discussed and to confirm any agreements that were made. This will help to ensure that everyone is on the same page and that the conversation was productive.

Difficult conversations can be challenging, but they can also be an opportunity to build relationships, resolve conflict, and improve the educational experience for everyone involved. By following these tips, you can effectively handle difficult conversations in education.

Here are some additional tips for dealing with difficult conversations in education:

- Choose the right time and place. Avoid having difficult conversations when you are feeling stressed or emotional. Choose a time and place where you can both focus on the conversation and where there will be no interruptions.

- Be clear and concise. Get to the point quickly and avoid rambling. The other person is more likely to listen to you if you are direct and to the point.

- Avoid personal attacks. Even if you are angry, it is important to avoid personal attacks. This will only make the situation worse.

- Be willing to walk away. If the conversation is becoming unproductive or if you feel like you are not being heard, be willing to walk away. This does not mean that you are giving up, it just means that you need to take a break and come back to the conversation when you are both calm.

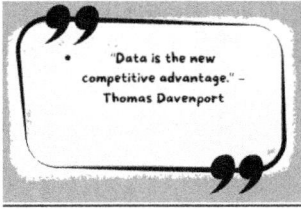

> • "Data is the new competitive advantage." – Thomas Davenport

The third chapter of the book discusses the importance of data-driven decision-making in school administration. . It covers topics such as:

- The importance of collecting data
- How to analyze data
- How to use data to make decisions
- How to avoid making decisions based on gut instinct

The importance of collecting data

Collecting data in education is important for a number of reasons. It can be used to:

- Identify areas for improvement. By collecting data on student achievement, attendance, and behavior, educators can identify areas where students are struggling and need additional support.

- Track student progress. Data can be used to track student progress over time, which can help educators identify which interventions are working and which ones need to be adjusted.

- Make decisions about instruction. Data can be used to make decisions about instruction, such as what topics to cover, what materials to use, and how to differentiate instruction for different learners.

- Hold schools accountable. Data can be used to hold schools accountable for student achievement. This can help ensure that all students have access to a high-quality education.

There are a number of ways to collect data in education. Some common methods include:

- Assessments: Assessments can be used to measure student achievement in a variety of subjects.

- Attendance records: Attendance records can be used to track student attendance and identify students who are at risk of dropping out.

- Behavior records: Behavior records can be used to track student behavior and identify students who are at risk of disciplinary action.

- Surveys: Surveys can be used to collect data from students, teachers, parents, and other stakeholders about their experiences with the school.

By collecting data in education, educators can make informed decisions about instruction, hold schools accountable, and improve the educational experience for all students.

Here are some additional benefits of collecting data in education:

- Data can be used to identify and close achievement gaps. By tracking student progress over time, educators can identify which students are falling behind and need additional support. This information can be used to develop interventions that can help close achievement gaps.

- Data can be used to improve teacher effectiveness. Data on student achievement can be used to identify which teachers are having the most success with their students. This information can be used to provide professional development to teachers who need it, and to reward teachers who are doing a good job.

- Data can be used to improve school climate. Data on student behavior can be used to identify which schools have a positive school climate, and which schools need to make changes to improve the climate. This information can be used to develop programs and policies that can improve the school climate for all students.

<u>How to analyze data</u>

Analyzing data in education is the process of collecting, organizing, and interpreting data to gain insights into student learning. This can be done using a variety of methods, including statistical analysis, data visualization, and storytelling.

There are many benefits to analyzing data in education. It can be used to:

- Identify areas for improvement. By analyzing data on student achievement, attendance, and behavior, educators can identify areas where students are struggling and need additional support.

- Track student progress. Data can be used to track student progress over time, which can help educators identify which interventions are working and which ones need to be adjusted.

- Make decisions about instruction. Data can be used to make decisions about instruction, such as what topics to cover, what materials to use, and how to differentiate instruction for different learners.

- Hold schools accountable. Data can be used to hold schools accountable for student achievement. This can help ensure that all students have access to a high-quality education.

There are a number of ways to analyze data in education. Some common methods include:

- Statistical analysis: Statistical analysis can be used to identify trends in data, such as whether students are making progress over time or whether there are differences in achievement between different groups of students.

- Data visualization: Data visualization can be used to present data in a way that is easy to understand, such as by creating charts, graphs, or maps.

- Storytelling: Storytelling can be used to share the findings of data analysis with a wider audience, such as by writing articles, giving presentations, or creating videos.

By analyzing data in education, educators can make informed decisions about instruction, hold schools accountable, and improve the educational experience for all students.

Here are some additional tips for analyzing data in education:

- Start with a clear goal. What do you hope to achieve by analyzing the data?

- Choose the right tools. There are a variety of tools available for analyzing data. Choose the tools that are right for your needs and your level of expertise.

- Clean the data. Before you can analyze the data, you need to make sure that it is clean and accurate. This may involve removing errors, correcting typos, and filling in missing data.

- Explore the data. Once the data is clean, you can start to explore it. Look for patterns, trends, and outliers.

- Interpret the data. Once you have explored the data, you need to interpret it. What does the data mean? What can you learn from it?

- Take action. Once you have interpreted the data, you need to take action. What changes can you make to improve student learning?

How to use data to make decisions

Using data to make decisions in education is a process of collecting, analyzing, and interpreting data to inform decisions about instruction, assessment, and other aspects of the educational environment. This process can be used to improve student learning, identify areas of need, and track progress over time.

There are many benefits to using data to make decisions in education. It can help educators:

- Identify areas for improvement: By analyzing data on student achievement, attendance, and behavior, educators can identify areas where students are struggling and need additional support.

- Track student progress: Data can be used to track student progress over time, which can help educators identify which interventions are working and which ones need to be adjusted.

- Make decisions about instruction: Data can be used to make decisions about instruction, such as what topics to cover, what materials to use, and how to differentiate instruction for different learners.

- Hold schools accountable: Data can be used to hold schools accountable for student achievement. This can help ensure that all students have access to a high-quality education.

There are a number of ways to use data to make decisions in education. Some common methods include:

- Data-driven decision making: This is a systematic approach to making decisions that is based on data. It involves collecting data, analyzing the data, and using the data to inform decisions.

- Evidence-based decision making: This is a decision-making process that is based on the best available evidence. It involves collecting and evaluating evidence, and using the evidence to inform decisions.

By using data to make decisions in education, educators can make informed decisions that are more likely to improve student learning.

Here are some additional tips for using data to make decisions in education:

- Start with a clear goal. What do you hope to achieve by using data?

- Choose the right data. Not all data is created equal. Choose data that is relevant to your goals and that is reliable and accurate.

- Analyze the data carefully. Don't just look at the numbers. Look for patterns, trends, and outliers.

- Interpret the data correctly. Don't make assumptions. Make sure you understand what the data is telling you.

- Take action. Once you have interpreted the data, you need to take action. What changes can you make to improve student learning?

How to avoid making decisions based on gut instinct

Gut instinct can be a helpful tool in decision-making, but it is important to avoid relying on it too heavily. Here are some tips for avoiding making decisions based on gut instinct in education:

1. Gather as much information as possible. Before making any decision, it is important to gather as much information as possible. This includes considering all of the relevant factors, such as the students' needs, the resources available, and the potential outcomes of the decision.

2. Consider the perspectives of others. It is also important to consider the perspectives of others, such as students, parents, teachers, and administrators. This can help to ensure that all of the relevant factors are considered and that the decision is in the best interests of all stakeholders.

3. Use data and evidence to support your decision. When making a decision, it is important to use data and evidence to support your decision. This can help to ensure that the decision is based on facts and not on gut instinct.

4. Be willing to change your mind. Even if you have gathered all of the information and considered the perspectives of others, it is still possible that you will make the wrong decision. Be willing to change your mind if new information comes to light or if the situation changes.

5. Reflect on your decision-making process. After you have made a decision, it is important to reflect on your decision-making process. This can help you to identify areas where you can improve your decision-making skills in the future.

By following these tips, you can avoid making decisions based on gut instinct and make more informed decisions that are in the best interests of all stakeholders.

Here are some additional tips for avoiding making decisions based on gut instinct in education:

- Be aware of your biases. Everyone has biases, and these biases can sometimes cloud our judgment. Be aware of your own biases and try to be as objective as possible when making decisions.

- Take the time to think things through. Don't rush into decisions. Take the time to think things through carefully and to consider all of the potential consequences.

- Get input from others. Don't make decisions in isolation. Get input from trusted advisors and colleagues.

- Be willing to change your mind. Even if you have done your research and considered all of the options, you may still need to change your mind in light of new information or changing circumstances.

Chapter 4: Budgeting and Finance

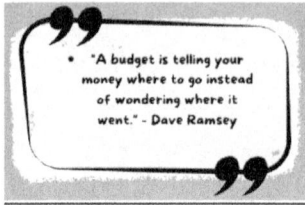

> "A budget is telling your money where to go instead of wondering where it went." - Dave Ramsey

The fourth chapter of the book discusses budgeting and finance in school administration. It covers topics such as:

- The importance of a sound financial plan
- How to create a budget
- How to track expenses
- How to manage cash flow
- How to raise money

The importance of a sound financial plan

A sound financial plan is important for any organization, but it is especially important for schools. Schools are facing increasing financial challenges, and a sound financial plan can help them to weather these challenges and ensure that they are able to continue to provide a high-quality education for their students.

Here are some of the benefits of having a sound financial plan in education:

- Improved decision-making: A sound financial plan provides schools with the information they need to make informed decisions about how to allocate their resources. This can help schools to ensure that they are using their money in the most effective way possible.

- Increased efficiency: A sound financial plan can help schools to identify areas where they can save money. This can help schools to reduce their costs and improve their efficiency.

- Enhanced financial stability: A sound financial plan can help schools to weather financial challenges. This can help schools to ensure that they are able to continue to provide a high-quality education for their students, even in difficult times.

Here are some tips for creating a sound financial plan for your school:

- Start by understanding your school's finances: The first step in creating a sound financial plan is to understand your school's finances. This includes understanding your school's revenue sources, your school's expenses, and your school's budget.

- Set realistic goals: Once you understand your school's finances, you need to set realistic goals for your school's financial plan. These goals should be based on your school's needs and your school's resources.

- Create a budget: Once you have set your goals, you need to create a budget. Your budget should outline how you plan to allocate your resources in order to achieve your goals.

- Monitor your progress: Once you have created your budget, you need to monitor your progress. This will help you to ensure that you are on track to achieve your goals.

- Make adjustments as needed: As your school's needs and resources change, you may need to make adjustments to your financial plan. This is perfectly normal. The important thing is to be proactive and to make adjustments as needed.

How to create a budget

A school budget is a financial plan that outlines how a school will use its resources to meet its goals. It includes revenue, expenses, and projections for the upcoming year.

Here are the steps on how to create a budget in schools:

1. Set goals. The first step is to set goals for the upcoming year. What do you want to achieve? What are your priorities?

2. Identify revenue sources. Once you know your goals, you need to identify your revenue sources. What are your sources of income?

3. Estimate expenses. Next, you need to estimate your expenses. What are your costs?

4. Create a budget. Once you have identified your revenue sources and estimated your expenses, you can create a budget. Your budget should outline how you plan to allocate your resources in order to achieve your goals.

5. Review and adjust your budget. Once you have created your budget, you need to review it and make adjustments as needed. This is important because your budget is a living document that should be updated as your needs and resources change.

6. Track your spending. Once you have finalized your budget, you need to track your spending. This will help you to ensure that you are staying on track and that you are not overspending.

7. Make adjustments as needed. As the school year progresses, you may need to make adjustments to your budget. This is normal. The important thing is to be proactive and to make adjustments as needed.

By following these steps, you can create a budget that will help you to achieve your goals and to provide a high-quality education for your students.

Here are some additional tips for creating a budget in schools:

- Be realistic. When estimating your expenses, be realistic. Don't underestimate your costs.

- Be flexible. Things change, so be prepared to make adjustments to your budget as needed.

- Get input from others. Don't create your budget in a vacuum. Get input from your staff, your students, and your parents.

- Use a budgeting software. There are many budgeting software programs available. These programs can help you to create and track your budget.

- Get help from a financial advisor. If you need help creating a budget, consider getting help from a financial advisor.

<u>How to track expenses</u>

Tracking expenses in schools can be a daunting task, but it is essential to ensure that funds are being used efficiently and effectively. There are a number of ways to track expenses in schools, including:

- Manual tracking: This involves manually recording all expenses in a spreadsheet or ledger. This can be time-consuming and prone to errors, but it is a good option for schools with limited resources.

- Software tracking: There are a number of software programs available that can help schools to track expenses. These programs can automate the process of tracking expenses and can provide reports that can help schools to identify areas where costs can be reduced.

- Hybrid tracking: This involves using a combination of manual and software tracking methods. This can be a good option for schools that want to take advantage of the benefits of both manual and software tracking.

No matter which method is chosen, it is important to ensure that all expenses are tracked accurately and efficiently. This will help schools to stay on budget and to make informed decisions about how to allocate resources.

Here are some tips for tracking expenses in schools:

- Establish a system: The first step is to establish a system for tracking expenses. This system should be clear and concise, and it should be easy for everyone to understand.

- Assign responsibility: Once a system has been established, it is important to assign responsibility for tracking expenses. This could be done by assigning a specific person or team to track expenses, or it could be done by requiring all staff members to track their own expenses.

- Use a tracking tool: There are a number of tracking tools available, including spreadsheets, software programs, and hybrid systems. The best tool for your school will depend on your needs and resources.

- Track all expenses: It is important to track all expenses, regardless of their size. This will help you to get a complete picture of your school's spending.

- Review expenses regularly: It is important to review expenses regularly. This will help you to identify areas where costs can be reduced or eliminated.

- Make adjustments as needed: As your school's needs and resources change, you may need to make adjustments to your expense tracking system. This is perfectly normal. The important thing is to be proactive and to make adjustments as needed.

By following these tips, you can track expenses in schools effectively. This will help your school to stay on budget and to make informed decisions about how to allocate resources.

Here are some additional tips for tracking expenses in schools:

- Get input from others: Don't track expenses in a vacuum. Get input from your staff, your students, and your parents.

- Use a budgeting software. There are many budgeting software programs available. These programs can help you to create and track your budget.

- Get help from a financial advisor. If you need help tracking expenses, consider getting help from a financial advisor.

How to manage cash flow

Managing cash flow in schools is essential to ensure that the school has enough money to cover its expenses. There are a number of ways to manage cash flow in schools, including:

- Creating a cash flow forecast: A cash flow forecast is a projection of how much money the school will have coming in and going out over a period of time. This can help the school to identify potential cash flow problems and to take steps to address them.

- Maintaining a healthy balance sheet: A balance sheet is a snapshot of the school's financial position at a given point in time. It shows the school's assets, liabilities, and equity. A healthy balance sheet indicates that the school has enough assets to cover its liabilities.

- Establishing a line of credit: A line of credit is a loan that can be used to cover short-term cash flow problems. This can be a helpful tool for schools that experience unexpected expenses or that have seasonal fluctuations in revenue.

- Managing accounts payable and receivables: Accounts payable are debts that the school owes to its vendors. Accounts receivable are payments that the school is owed by its customers. Managing accounts payable and receivables effectively can help the school to improve its cash flow.

- Investing excess cash: When a school has excess cash, it can invest it in a variety of ways, such as in short-term investments, long-term investments, or endowments. This can help the school to earn interest on its cash and to grow its financial reserves.

By following these tips, schools can manage cash flow effectively and ensure that they have enough money to cover their expenses.

Here are some additional tips for managing cash flow in schools:

- Be proactive: Don't wait until there is a cash flow problem to take action. Be proactive and monitor your cash flow on a regular basis.

- Communicate with stakeholders: Keep your stakeholders, such as your staff, your students, and your parents, informed about your cash flow situation. This will help to build trust and confidence.

- Get help from a financial advisor: If you need help managing your cash flow, consider getting help from a financial advisor.

How to raise money

Here are some ideas on how to raise money in schools:

- Hold a school fundraiser: There are many different types of school fundraisers, such as bake sales, car washes, and silent auctions. You can also hold a school-wide event such as a talent show or a sporting event, and charge admission.

- Get involved in community events: There are many community events that you can participate in to raise money for your school. For example, you can volunteer at a local food bank or participate in a community 5K run.

- Start a crowdfunding campaign: Crowdfunding is a great way to raise money for your school. You can create a crowdfunding campaign on a platform like GoFundMe or Kickstarter.

- Reach out to local businesses: Local businesses may be willing to donate money or goods to your school. You can reach out to businesses in your community and ask for their support.

- Apply for grants: There are many grants available to schools. You can research grants that are available to your school and apply for them.

When choosing a fundraising method, it is important to consider the following factors:

- The cost of the fundraiser: Some fundraising methods, such as bake sales and car washes, are relatively inexpensive to organize. Other fundraising methods, such as silent auctions and sporting events, can be more expensive.

- The time commitment required: Some fundraising methods, such as bake sales and car washes, can be organized and executed relatively quickly. Other fundraising methods, such as silent auctions and sporting events, can require more time and planning.

- The potential for success: Some fundraising methods, such as bake sales and car washes, have a proven track record of success. Other fundraising methods, such as silent auctions and sporting events, may be more risky.

By considering these factors, you can choose a fundraising method that is right for your school.

Here are some additional tips for raising money in schools:

- Get everyone involved: The more people who are involved in fundraising, the more successful it will be. Get students, parents, teachers, and staff involved in planning and executing fundraising events.
- Be creative: There are many different ways to raise money. Get creative and come up with ideas that will appeal to your community.
- Be persistent: Fundraising can be challenging, but it is important to be persistent. Don't give up if you don't reach your goals right away. Keep working hard and you will eventually reach your goals.

Chapter 5: Human Resources

> "The most important thing in business is to hire the right people and then give them the opportunity to do what they want to do."
> - David Packard

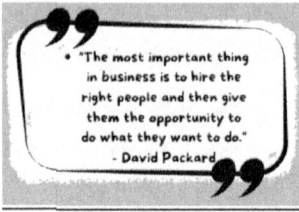

The fifth chapter of the book discusses human resources in school administration. It covers topics such as:

- The importance of hiring the right people
- How to develop and train employees
- How to create a positive work environment
- How to deal with employee performance issues

The importance of hiring the right people

Hiring the right people in schools is essential to ensuring that students receive a high-quality education. The wrong hiring decisions can have a negative impact on student achievement, school culture, and staff morale.

Here are some of the reasons why it is important to hire the right people in schools:

- To ensure that students receive a high-quality education. The quality of education that students receive is directly related to the quality of the teachers and staff who work in their schools. The right people can make a real difference in the lives of students, helping them to learn and grow.

- To create a positive school culture. The school culture is the overall atmosphere of a school, and it is created by the people who work there. The right people can create a positive school culture that is conducive to learning and growth.

- To boost staff morale. Staff morale is important for a number of reasons, including student achievement, school climate, and retention. The right people can boost staff morale and create a more positive work environment.

Here are some tips for hiring the right people in schools:

- Define the role and responsibilities. Before you start looking for candidates, it is important to define the role and responsibilities of the position. This will help you to identify the skills and experience that you are looking for in a candidate.

- Create a job description. A job description is a written document that outlines the role and responsibilities of a position. It should also include the skills and experience that you are looking for in a candidate.

- Use a variety of hiring methods. There are a number of different ways to hire people, including online job postings, networking, and employee referrals. Using a variety of hiring methods will help you to reach a wider pool of candidates.

- Conduct interviews. Interviews are an important part of the hiring process. They allow you to get to know the candidates and to assess their skills and experience.

- Check references. Checking references is another important part of the hiring process. It allows you to get feedback from people who have worked with the candidates in the past.

- Make an offer. Once you have found the right person, it is time to make an offer. The offer should include the salary, benefits, and start date.

- Onboard the new employee. Onboarding is the process of integrating a new employee into the organization. It should include introducing the employee to their new colleagues, providing them with training, and helping them to get settled into their new role.

How to develop and train employees

Here are some tips on how to develop and train employees in schools:

- Set clear goals and expectations. Before you start any training program, it is important to set clear goals and expectations. What do you want employees to learn? What skills do you want them to develop? Once you know what you want to achieve, you can start to develop a training program that will meet your needs.

- Provide regular feedback. Feedback is essential for employee development. It helps employees to identify their strengths and weaknesses, and it helps them to track their progress. Provide regular feedback to employees, both positive and negative.

- Offer opportunities for professional development. Professional development is a great way for employees to learn new skills and stay up-to-date on the latest trends in their field. Offer employees opportunities for professional development, such as attending conferences, taking online courses, or mentoring other employees.

- Create a culture of continuous learning. A culture of continuous learning is an environment where employees are encouraged to learn and grow. This can be achieved by providing employees with opportunities for professional development, by creating a supportive work environment, and by celebrating employee achievements.

- Recognize and reward employee achievements. When employees achieve their goals, it is important to recognize and reward their achievements. This will help to motivate employees to continue to learn and grow. Recognition and rewards can take many forms, such as public praise, bonuses, or time off.

By following these tips, you can create a culture of continuous learning in your school and help employees to develop the skills they need to be successful.

Here are some additional tips for developing and training employees in schools:

- Tailor training to the individual. Not all employees learn in the same way, so it is important to tailor training to the individual. Some employees may prefer to learn by reading, while others may prefer to learn by doing.

- Make training relevant to the job. Employees are more likely to retain information if they can see how it is relevant to their job. Make sure that training is relevant to the employee's role and responsibilities.

- Make training fun and engaging. Training should be fun and engaging. This will help to keep employees motivated and interested in learning.

- Provide opportunities for practice. Employees need opportunities to practice what they have learned. This will help them to solidify their knowledge and skills.

- Provide support and encouragement. Employees need support and encouragement throughout the training process. This will help them to overcome challenges and stay motivated.

How to create a positive work environment

Here are some tips on how to create a positive work environment in schools:

- Encourage open communication and collaboration. A positive work environment is one where employees feel comfortable communicating with each other and collaborating on projects. Encourage open communication by creating a culture of trust and respect.

- Provide opportunities for professional development. Employees who feel like they are constantly learning and growing are more likely to be engaged and productive. Provide opportunities for professional development by offering trainings, workshops, and conferences.

- Celebrate successes. When employees achieve their goals, it is important to celebrate their successes. This will help to motivate employees and create a sense of community.

- Be fair and consistent. Employees want to feel like they are treated fairly and consistently. Be sure to set clear expectations and follow through on consequences.

- Provide a safe and supportive environment. A positive work environment is one where employees feel safe and supported. This means creating a physical environment that is free from hazards and a culture that is free from discrimination and harassment.

By following these tips, you can create a positive work environment in your school. This will help to improve employee morale, productivity, and retention.

Here are some additional tips for creating a positive work environment in schools:

- Be approachable. Employees should feel comfortable coming to you with questions or concerns. Make yourself available to employees and let them know that you are there to support them.

- Be flexible. Things don't always go according to plan, so it's important to be flexible and willing to adapt. Be understanding when employees need to take time off or make changes to their schedules.

- Be positive. A positive attitude can go a long way in creating a positive work environment. Be sure to express your appreciation for employees' hard work and let them know that you are confident in their abilities.

How to deal with employee performance issues

Here are some tips on how to deal with employee performance issues in schools:

- Assess the situation. The first step is to assess the situation and determine the nature of the performance issue. Is the employee consistently late for work? Are they not meeting their performance goals? Are they disruptive in the workplace? Once you have a better understanding of the issue, you can start to develop a plan to address it.

- Meet with the employee. Once you have assessed the situation, it is important to meet with the employee to discuss the issue. Be clear and direct about the performance issue and the impact it is having on the school. Be willing to listen to the employee's perspective and work together to develop a plan to improve their performance.

- Provide support and resources. If the employee is struggling with a performance issue, it may be helpful to provide them with support and resources. This could include providing them with training, mentoring, or counseling.

- Document the situation. It is important to document all meetings and conversations with the employee. This will help to protect the school if the issue escalates.

- Take disciplinary action if necessary. If the employee's performance does not improve, it may be necessary to take disciplinary action. This could include a warning, suspension, or termination.

It is important to remember that every situation is different. The best way to deal with employee performance issues is to be fair, consistent, and supportive.

Here are some additional tips for dealing with employee performance issues in schools:

- Be objective. When assessing an employee's performance, it is important to be objective and to focus on the facts. Avoid making assumptions or judgments about the employee's motives.

- Be respectful. Even when dealing with a difficult employee, it is important to be respectful. Remember that the employee is a human being and that they deserve to be treated with dignity and respect.

- Be patient. It may take time for an employee to improve their performance. Be patient and supportive, and offer the employee the resources they need to succeed.

> "Facilities management is the art of making the best use of people, space, and money." – James A. O'Brien

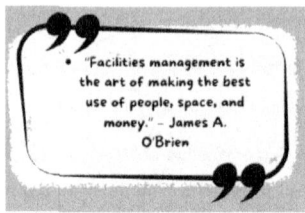

The sixth chapter of the book discusses facilities management in school administration. It covers topics such as:

- The importance of maintaining school facilities
- How to manage repairs and maintenance
- How to create a safe and secure environment
- How to comply with safety regulations

The importance of maintaining school facilities

Maintaining school facilities is important for a number of reasons, including:

- To ensure the safety of students and staff. A well-maintained school facility is a safe school facility. This means that there are no hazards, such as broken glass or uneven floors, that could cause injury.

- To improve the learning environment. A clean and well-maintained school facility is a more inviting and conducive learning environment. This can lead to improved student achievement.

- To extend the life of the building. Regular maintenance can help to extend the life of a school building. This can save the school district money in the long run.

- To improve the school's image. A well-maintained school facility makes a positive impression on the community. This can help to attract new students and families.

Here are some tips for maintaining school facilities:

- Create a maintenance plan. A maintenance plan is a schedule of tasks that need to be performed on a regular basis. This will help to ensure that the school facility is properly maintained.

- Assign tasks to staff members. The tasks in the maintenance plan should be assigned to staff members who are qualified to perform them.

- Provide training to staff members. Staff members who are responsible for maintenance should be trained on how to perform the tasks safely and effectively.

- Keep records of maintenance activities. Records of maintenance activities should be kept so that problems can be identified and addressed in a timely manner.

- Budget for maintenance. A budget should be set aside for maintenance so that the school district can afford to keep the school facility in good condition.

By following these tips, schools can ensure that their facilities are properly maintained and that students and staff are safe.

Here are some additional tips for maintaining school facilities:

- Encourage students and staff to report any problems. Students and staff are often the first to notice problems with a school facility. Encourage them to report any problems so that they can be addressed quickly.

- Be proactive. Don't wait for problems to occur before taking action. Be proactive and inspect the school facility on a regular basis to identify and address potential problems.

- Use the right tools and materials. When performing maintenance, use the right tools and materials. This will help to ensure that the work is done correctly and that the school facility is not damaged.

- Follow safety procedures. Always follow safety procedures when performing maintenance. This will help to prevent injuries.

<u>How to manage repairs and maintenance</u>

Managing repairs and maintenance in schools can be a challenge, but it is important to ensure that school facilities are safe and in good condition. Here are some tips for managing repairs and maintenance in schools:

- Create a maintenance plan. A maintenance plan is a schedule of tasks that need to be performed on a regular basis. This will help to ensure that the school facility is properly maintained.

- Assign tasks to staff members. The tasks in the maintenance plan should be assigned to staff members who are qualified to perform them.

- Provide training to staff members. Staff members who are responsible for maintenance should be trained on how to perform the tasks safely and effectively.

- Keep records of maintenance activities. Records of maintenance activities should be kept so that problems can be identified and addressed in a timely manner.

- Budget for maintenance. A budget should be set aside for maintenance so that the school district can afford to keep the school facility in good condition.

- Use a maintenance management software. A maintenance management software can help to track maintenance tasks, costs, and schedules. This can help to improve efficiency and save time.

Here are some additional tips for managing repairs and maintenance in schools:

- Encourage students and staff to report any problems. Students and staff are often the first to notice problems with a school facility. Encourage them to report any problems so that they can be addressed quickly.

- Be proactive. Don't wait for problems to occur before taking action. Be proactive and inspect the school facility on a regular basis to identify and address potential problems.

- Use the right tools and materials. When performing maintenance, use the right tools and materials. This will help to ensure that the work is done correctly and that the school facility is not damaged.

- Follow safety procedures. Always follow safety procedures when performing maintenance. This will help to prevent injuries.

By following these tips, schools can ensure that their facilities are properly maintained and that students and staff are safe.

Here are some of the benefits of managing repairs and maintenance in schools:

- Improved safety: By keeping school facilities in good condition, schools can help to prevent accidents and injuries.

- Improved learning environment: A clean and well-maintained school facility is a more inviting and conducive learning environment. This can lead to improved student achievement.

- Extended life of the building: Regular maintenance can help to extend the life of a school building. This can save the school district money in the long run.

- Improved school image: A well-maintained school facility makes a positive impression on the community. This can help to attract new students and families.

How to create a safe and secure environment

Creating a safe and secure environment in schools is essential for the well-being of students, staff, and the community. There are a number of things that schools can do to create a safe and secure environment, including:

- Developing a school safety plan. A school safety plan is a document that outlines the steps that a school will take to prevent and respond to safety incidents. The plan should be developed by a team of stakeholders, including students, staff, parents, and community members.

- Implementing security measures. Security measures can help to deter crime and violence on school grounds. Some common security measures include:

o Installing security cameras

- Hiring security guards

- Conducting regular safety drills

- Creating a system for reporting suspicious activity

- Providing training to staff and students. Staff and students should be trained on how to identify and respond to potential safety threats. Training should cover topics such as:

- How to identify and report suspicious activity

- How to de-escalate conflict

- How to respond to an emergency

- Creating a culture of respect and inclusion. A school culture that is based on respect and inclusion can help to prevent bullying and harassment. Schools can create a culture of respect and inclusion by:

- Promoting positive relationships between students, staff, and parents

- Developing clear policies on bullying and harassment

- Providing training on how to prevent and respond to bullying and harassment

- Communicating with the community. Schools should communicate with the community about safety issues. This can be done through newsletters, community meetings, and social media. By communicating with the community, schools can build trust and support for their safety efforts.

By taking these steps, schools can create a safe and secure environment for students, staff, and the community.

Here are some additional tips for creating a safe and secure environment in schools:

- Be proactive. Don't wait for problems to occur before taking action. Be proactive and identify potential safety threats and take steps to address them.

- Be visible. The presence of staff and security can help to deter crime and violence. Make sure that staff and security are visible throughout the school day.

- Be responsive. If a safety incident does occur, be responsive and take steps to investigate the incident and prevent it from happening again.

- Be supportive. Students, staff, and parents should feel supported by the school community. Provide support to those who have been affected by a safety incident.

How to comply with safety regulations

Schools have a legal responsibility to ensure the safety of their students and staff. This includes complying with all applicable safety regulations. Here are some tips on how to comply with safety regulations in schools:

- Develop a safety policy. A safety policy is a document that outlines the school's commitment to safety and the steps that the school will take to protect students and staff. The policy should be developed by a team of stakeholders, including students, staff, parents, and community members.

- Identify hazards. The first step in complying with safety regulations is to identify the hazards that exist in the school environment. This can be done by conducting a hazard assessment. A hazard assessment is a process of identifying and evaluating potential hazards in the school environment.

- Assess risks. Once the hazards have been identified, the next step is to assess the risks associated with each hazard. Risk assessment is a process of determining the likelihood and severity of harm that could occur from a hazard.

- Implement controls. Once the risks have been assessed, the next step is to implement controls to reduce or eliminate the risks. Controls can include engineering controls, administrative controls, and personal protective equipment.

- Train staff and students. All staff and students should be trained on the school's safety policy and the procedures for identifying and responding to hazards. Training should be ongoing and should be tailored to the specific needs of the school.

- Monitor and evaluate. The school should monitor and evaluate its safety program on a regular basis to ensure that it is effective. Monitoring and evaluation can help to identify areas where the program can be improved.

By following these tips, schools can comply with safety regulations and create a safe and healthy environment for students and staff.

Here are some additional tips for complying with safety regulations in schools:

- Keep records. Schools should keep records of all safety-related incidents, including accidents, injuries, and near misses. This information can be used to identify trends and to develop strategies for preventing future incidents.

- Report incidents. Schools should report all safety-related incidents to the appropriate authorities, such as the local fire department or health department. This helps to ensure that the community is aware of the risks and that steps can be taken to mitigate them.

- Work with the community. Schools should work with the community to develop and implement safety programs. This can be done by forming a safety committee that includes representatives from the school, the community, and local businesses.

- Be proactive. Don't wait for problems to occur before taking action. Be proactive and identify potential safety hazards and take steps to address them.

Chapter 7: Risk Management

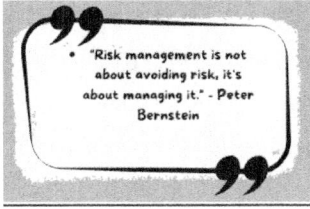

> • "Risk management is not about avoiding risk, it's about managing it." - Peter Bernstein

The seventh chapter of the book discusses risk management in school administration. This covers topics such as:

- The importance of identifying and managing risks
- How to develop a risk management plan
- How to respond to incidents
- How to mitigate future risks

The importance of identifying and managing risks

Schools are responsible for the safety of their students and staff. This includes identifying and managing risks that could potentially harm them. Here are some of the reasons why it is important to identify and manage risks in schools:

- To protect students and staff. The most important reason to identify and manage risks is to protect students and staff from harm. By identifying and addressing potential risks, schools can help to prevent accidents, injuries, and other incidents that could cause harm.
- To comply with regulations. Schools have a legal responsibility to comply with all applicable safety regulations. By identifying and managing risks, schools can help to ensure that they are meeting their legal obligations.
- To reduce liability. By identifying and managing risks, schools can help to reduce their liability exposure. If an accident or injury does occur, schools that have a

comprehensive risk management program in place may be able to defend themselves against lawsuits.

- To improve morale. A safe and secure environment is essential for a positive school climate. By identifying and managing risks, schools can help to create a safe and secure environment that will promote student learning and staff morale.

Here are some of the risks that schools should be aware of:

- Accidents. Accidents are the most common type of risk in schools. They can be caused by a variety of factors, such as slips, trips, and falls.

- Violence. Violence is a serious risk in schools. It can be caused by bullying, gang activity, or other factors.

- Health hazards. Health hazards can include exposure to asbestos, lead, or other harmful substances.

- Natural disasters. Natural disasters, such as floods, earthquakes, and hurricanes, can pose a risk to schools.

There are a number of things that schools can do to identify and manage risks. Here are some examples:

- Conduct hazard assessments. A hazard assessment is a process of identifying and evaluating potential hazards in the school environment.

- Develop safety policies and procedures. Safety policies and procedures should outline the school's commitment to safety and the steps that the school will take to protect students and staff.

- Provide training. All staff and students should be trained on the school's safety policies and procedures.

- Implement controls. Controls can be implemented to reduce or eliminate risks. Controls can include engineering controls, administrative controls, and personal protective equipment.

• Monitor and evaluate. The school should monitor and evaluate its safety program on a regular basis to ensure that it is effective.

How to develop a risk management plan

Risk management is the process of identifying, assessing, and managing risks. A risk management plan is a document that outlines the steps that a school will take to identify, assess, and manage risks.

Here are the steps on how to develop a risk management plan in schools:

1. Establish a risk management team. The risk management team should be composed of representatives from various departments within the school, such as administration, facilities, safety, and health.

2. Identify risks. The risk management team should identify all potential risks to students and staff. This can be done by conducting a hazard assessment. A hazard assessment is a process of identifying and evaluating potential hazards in the school environment.

3. Assess risks. Once the risks have been identified, the risk management team should assess the risks associated with each hazard. Risk assessment is a process of determining the likelihood and severity of harm that could occur from a hazard.

4. Develop risk control measures. Once the risks have been assessed, the risk management team should develop risk control measures to reduce or eliminate the risks. Risk control measures can include engineering controls, administrative controls, and personal protective equipment.

5. Implement risk control measures. The risk management team should implement the risk control measures that have been developed.

6. Monitor and evaluate risk control measures. The risk management team should monitor and evaluate the effectiveness of the risk control measures that have been implemented.

7. Review and update the risk management plan. The risk management plan should be reviewed and updated on a regular basis to ensure that it is effective.

Here are some tips for developing a risk management plan in schools:

- Get everyone involved. The risk management plan should be developed with input from all stakeholders, including students, staff, parents, and community members.

- Be proactive. Don't wait for problems to occur before taking action. Be proactive and identify potential risks and take steps to address them.

- Be realistic. Don't try to eliminate all risks. Some risks are unavoidable. However, you can reduce the likelihood and severity of harm by implementing risk control measures.

- Be flexible. The risk management plan should be flexible enough to be updated as new risks are identified and as the school environment changes.

How to respond to incidents

Here are some tips on how to respond to incidents in schools:

- Stay calm. It is important to stay calm in the event of an incident. This will help you to think clearly and make sound decisions.

- Assess the situation. Once you have stayed calm, assess the situation. This will help you to determine the severity of the incident and the best course of action.

- Take action. Once you have assessed the situation, take action. This may involve calling for help, evacuating the building, or providing first aid.

- Communicate with others. Once you have taken action, communicate with others. This may involve informing parents, staff, or the police.

- Provide support. Once the incident has been resolved, provide support to those who have been affected. This may involve providing counseling or other services.

Here are some additional tips on how to respond to incidents in schools:

- Be prepared. Schools should have a plan in place for responding to incidents. This plan should be developed with input from all stakeholders, including students, staff, parents, and community members.

- Train staff. All staff should be trained on how to respond to incidents. This training should cover topics such as:

  o How to identify and report incidents

  o How to stay calm in an emergency

  o How to provide first aid

  o How to communicate with others

- Have a communication plan. Schools should have a communication plan in place for communicating with parents and the community in the event of an incident. This plan should include information on how to contact the school, how to get updates on the situation, and how to provide support to those who have been affected.

- Be flexible. No two incidents are the same, so it is important to be flexible in your response. The best course of action may vary depending on the specific circumstances of the incident.

How to mitigate future risks

Mitigating future risks in schools can be done by taking a number of steps, including:

- Identifying potential risks. The first step is to identify all potential risks to students and staff. This can be done by conducting a hazard assessment. A hazard assessment is a process of identifying and evaluating potential hazards in the school environment.

- Assess risks. Once the risks have been identified, the next step is to assess the risks associated with each hazard. Risk assessment is a process of determining the likelihood and severity of harm that could occur from a hazard.

- Develop risk control measures. Once the risks have been assessed, the next step is to develop risk control measures to reduce or eliminate the risks. Risk control measures can include engineering controls, administrative controls, and personal protective equipment.

- Implement risk control measures. The next step is to implement the risk control measures that have been developed.

- Monitor and evaluate risk control measures. The next step is to monitor and evaluate the effectiveness of the risk control measures that have been implemented.

- Review and update the risk management plan. The final step is to review and update the risk management plan on a regular basis to ensure that it is effective.

Here are some additional tips for mitigating future risks in schools:

- Get everyone involved. The risk management plan should be developed with input from all stakeholders, including students, staff, parents, and community members.

- Be proactive. Don't wait for problems to occur before taking action. Be proactive and identify potential risks and take steps to address them.

- Be realistic. Don't try to eliminate all risks. Some risks are unavoidable. However, you can reduce the likelihood and severity of harm by implementing risk control measures.

- Be flexible. The risk management plan should be flexible enough to be updated as new risks are identified and as the school environment changes.

By following these steps, schools can mitigate future risks and create a safe and secure environment for students and staff.

Here are some specific examples of how schools can mitigate future risks:

- Accidents: Schools can mitigate the risk of accidents by installing safety equipment, such as guardrails and floor mats, and by providing training on safety procedures.

- Violence: Schools can mitigate the risk of violence by hiring security guards, installing security cameras, and developing a school safety plan.

- Health hazards: Schools can mitigate the risk of health hazards by conducting regular inspections of the school environment, testing for hazardous substances, and providing training on health and safety procedures.

- Natural disasters: Schools can mitigate the risk of natural disasters by developing a disaster plan, conducting regular drills, and securing the school building.

Chapter 8: Compliance

> "Compliance is not just about following the rules, it's about doing the right thing."

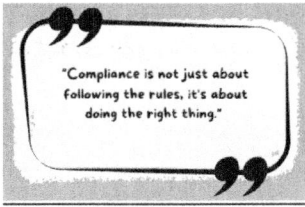

The eighth chapter of the book discusses compliance in school administration. It covers topics such as:

- The importance of complying with regulations
- How to identify and understand regulations
- How to develop a compliance plan
- How to monitor compliance

The importance of complying with regulations

Complying with regulations in schools is important for a number of reasons, including:

- To protect students and staff. Regulations are designed to protect students and staff from harm. By complying with regulations, schools can help to ensure the safety of their students and staff.

- To comply with the law. Schools have a legal responsibility to comply with all applicable regulations. By failing to comply with regulations, schools could be subject to legal action.

- To maintain public trust. When schools comply with regulations, it helps to maintain public trust. Parents, students, and the community want to know that their schools are safe and that they are following the law.

- To improve school performance. By complying with regulations, schools can improve their performance. For example, schools that comply with regulations on bullying and harassment are more likely to have a positive school climate.

Here are some of the regulations that schools must comply with:

- Health and safety regulations. These regulations are designed to protect students and staff from harm. They cover a wide range of topics, including fire safety, food safety, and personal protective equipment.

- Education regulations. These regulations are designed to ensure that students are receiving a quality education. They cover a wide range of topics, including curriculum, instruction, and assessment.

- Civil rights regulations. These regulations are designed to protect students from discrimination. They cover a wide range of topics, including race, religion, and disability.

Schools can comply with regulations by:

- Developing policies and procedures. Schools should develop policies and procedures that are in line with the regulations.

- Training staff. All staff should be trained on the school's policies and procedures.

- Monitoring compliance. The school should monitor compliance with its policies and procedures.

- Taking corrective action. If the school finds that it is not in compliance with regulations, it should take corrective action.

By complying with regulations, schools can help to create a safe and supportive environment for students and staff. They can also improve their performance and maintain public trust.

How to identify and understand regulations

Here are some tips on how to identify and understand regulations in schools:

- Talk to your school administrator. Your school administrator is responsible for ensuring that the school complies with all applicable regulations. They can help you to identify the regulations that apply to your school and to understand what the regulations require.

- Read the regulations. The regulations are usually available on the school's website or in the school's library. If you have trouble understanding the regulations, you can ask your school administrator for help.

- Talk to your union representative. If you are a teacher or other school employee, you may have a union representative. Your union representative can help you to understand the regulations and to advocate for your rights.

- Get training. Your school may offer training on the regulations. If not, you can find training online or through a professional organization.

- Stay up-to-date. The regulations are constantly changing. You can stay up-to-date by reading the school's website or by subscribing to a newsletter or blog that covers education law.

By following these tips, you can help to ensure that your school is complying with all applicable regulations.

Here are some additional tips for identifying and understanding regulations in schools:

- Be proactive. Don't wait for problems to occur before taking action. Be proactive and identify potential regulatory issues and take steps to address them.

- Be realistic. Don't try to comply with all regulations at once. Start with the most important regulations and work your way down the list.

- Be flexible. The regulations are not always clear-cut. Be prepared to interpret the regulations in a way that is fair and reasonable.

- Be open to feedback. Get feedback from your colleagues, students, parents, and the community. This will help you to identify any areas where you need to improve your compliance efforts.

How to develop a compliance plan

Here are some steps on how to develop a compliance plan in schools:

1. Identify the regulations. The first step is to identify all of the regulations that apply to your school. This can be done by talking to your school administrator, reading the regulations, talking to your union representative, getting training, and staying up-to-date.

2. Assess the risks. Once you have identified the regulations, you need to assess the risks associated with non-compliance. This will help you to determine which regulations are most important to focus on.

3. Develop policies and procedures. The next step is to develop policies and procedures that will help you to comply with the regulations. These policies and procedures should be clear, concise, and easy to understand.

4. Train staff. All staff should be trained on the school's policies and procedures. This training should be ongoing and should be updated as new regulations are issued or as the school's policies and procedures change.

5. Monitor compliance. The school should monitor compliance with its policies and procedures. This can be done through self-assessments, audits, and investigations.

6. Take corrective action. If the school finds that it is not in compliance with a regulation, it should take corrective action. This may involve changing its policies and procedures, providing training, or disciplining staff.

By following these steps, you can help to ensure that your school is in compliance with all applicable regulations.

Here are some additional tips for developing a compliance plan in schools:

- Get buy-in from the school administration. The school administration must be committed to compliance in order for the compliance plan to be successful.

- Involve all stakeholders. All stakeholders, including students, parents, staff, and the community, should be involved in the development and implementation of the compliance plan.

- Make it easy to comply. The compliance plan should be easy to understand and follow.

- Be flexible. The compliance plan should be flexible enough to be updated as new regulations are issued or as the school's environment changes.

- Be proactive. Don't wait for problems to occur before taking action. Be proactive and identify potential compliance issues and take steps to address them.

How to monitor compliance

Here are some ways to monitor compliance in schools:

- Self-assessments. Schools can conduct self-assessments to identify areas where they may not be in compliance with regulations. Self-assessments can be done by staff, students, parents, or a combination of all three.

- Audits. External audits can be conducted by a third party to assess the school's compliance with regulations. Audits can be comprehensive or focused on specific areas of concern.

- Investigations. Investigations can be conducted by the school or by a government agency to look into allegations of non-compliance. Investigations can be triggered by complaints, tips, or other information.

By monitoring compliance, schools can identify and address any areas where they may not be in compliance with regulations. This can help to prevent problems from occurring and to protect students and staff.

Here are some additional tips for monitoring compliance in schools:

- Create a culture of compliance. The school should create a culture of compliance where everyone is aware of the regulations and is committed to following them.
- Have a clear reporting system. The school should have a clear reporting system in place so that staff, students, and parents can report any concerns about compliance.
- Take corrective action promptly. If the school finds that it is not in compliance with a regulation, it should take corrective action promptly. This may involve changing its policies and procedures, providing training, or disciplining staff.

By following these tips, schools can help to ensure that they are in compliance with all applicable regulations.

Here are some of the benefits of monitoring compliance in schools:

- Increased safety. By monitoring compliance with safety regulations, schools can help to create a safer environment for students and staff.
- Improved educational outcomes. By monitoring compliance with education regulations, schools can help to ensure that all students are receiving a quality education.
- Reduced liability. By monitoring compliance with all applicable regulations, schools can reduce their risk of being sued.
- Improved public trust. By demonstrating a commitment to compliance, schools can improve public trust and confidence.

Resources

The book includes lists of resources for further information, including websites, books, and articles. These are by no means endorsed by the author, results where provided by Google search.

About the Author

The book was written by an experienced school administrator with over 20 years of experience in the field of management and improvement. The author has a proven record of accomplishment of improving school administration and has a deep understanding of the challenges and opportunities facing school leaders today.

Conclusion

This book provides a comprehensive guide to improving school administration by providing informative, clear and simple guidance. It is a valuable resource for school leaders and administrators who are looking to improve the performance of their schools. The conclusion of the book summarizes the key points of the book and provides a call to action for school leaders and administrators. We hope you have enjoyed reading this book and can use it for your study and everyday work life.

I hope that this book has been helpful in sharing my knowledge and experience with you. I have tried to cover a wide range of topics, from the importance of sharing knowledge to the different ways to do it. I hope that you will find this information useful and that it will inspire you to share your own knowledge and experience with others.

Sharing knowledge is a powerful thing. It can help us to learn, to grow, and to make a difference in the world. It is also a lot of fun! So please, do not be afraid to share your knowledge with others. The world needs it.

Thank you for reading

@RedTape27 – John Evans M.Ed, MAAT, CMgr MCMI

This book would not have been possible if it was not for support of my wife and children, so thank you Stacey, Lillie and Sophie.

Bibliography

Alsharef, A., Banerjee, S., Uddin, S.J., Albert, A. and Jaselskis, E., 2021. Early impacts of the COVID-19 pandemic on the United States construction industry. International journal of environmental research and public health, 18(4), p.1559.

Andersen, J.A., 2006. Leadership, personality and effectiveness. The journal of socio-economics, 35(6), pp.1078-1091.

Ashkanasy, N.M., Ayoko, O.B. and Jehn, K.A., 2014. Understanding the physical environment of work and employee behavior: An affective events perspective. Journal of Organizational Behavior, 35(8), pp.1169-1184.

Atolia, M., Li, B.G., Marto, R. and Melina, M.G., 2017. Investing in public infrastructure: Roads or schools?. International Monetary Fund.

Barker, 2022. Impact of Rising Energy Costs on Education. Available at https://www.barker-associates.co.uk/insights/impact-of-rising-energy-costs-on-education/ [Accessed 8th August 2022].

Barrett, P.S., Zhang, Y., Davies, F. and Barrett, L.C., 2015. Clever classrooms: Summary report of the HEAD project. University of Salford.

Behling, O. and Law, K.S., 2000. Translating questionnaires and other research instruments: Problems and solutions (Vol. 133). sage.

Bencivenga, M. and Camocini, B., 2022. 5. Post-pandemic scenarios of office workplace: new purposes of the physical spaces to enhance social and individual well-being. DESIGNING BEHAVIOURS FOR WELL-BEING SPACES.

Blumberg, B., Cooper, D. and Schindler, P., 2014. EBOOK: Business Research Methods. McGraw Hill.

Boland, B., De Smet, A., Palter, R. and Sanghvi, A., 2020. Reimagining the office and work life after COVID-19.

Bonner, A. and Tolhurst, G., 2002. Insider-outsider perspectives of participant observation. Nurse Researcher (through 2013), 9(4), p.7.

Brenner, D.A., 2007. Achieving a successful project by motivating the project team. Cost Engineering, 49(5), p.16.

Brookes, M.J. and Kaplan, A., 1972. The office environment: Space planning and affective behavior. Human factors, 14(5), pp.373-391.

Bueno, S., Rodríguez-Baltanás, G. and Gallego, M.D., 2018. Coworking spaces: A new way of achieving productivity. Journal of Facilities Management.

Burman, E., Kimpian, J. and Mumovic, D., 2018. Building schools for the future: lessons learned from performance evaluations of five secondary schools and academies in England. Frontiers in Built Environment, 4, p.22.

Cacciattolo, M., 2015. Ethical considerations in research. In The Praxis of English Language Teaching and Learning (PELT) (pp. 55-73). Brill.

Chambers, D., 2015. The changing nature of the roles of support staff. In Working with teaching assistants and other support staff for inclusive education. Emerald Group Publishing Limited.

Cipolla, Z., Diaz, E., Hansen, N., McGann, L., Nardone, M. and Rawson, F., 2022. Global Program for Safer Schools (GPSS).

Colenberg, S., Jylhä, T. and Arkesteijn, M., 2021. The relationship between interior office space and employee health and well-being–a literature review. *Building Research & Information*, *49*(3), pp.352-366.

Cramer, D., 2003. Advanced quantitative data analysis. McGraw-Hill Education (UK).

Da, S., Fladmark, S.F., Wara, I., Christensen, M. and Innstrand, S.T., 2022. To change or not to change: A study of workplace change during the COVID-19 pandemic. International Journal of Environmental Research and Public Health, 19(4), p.1982.

Danielsson, C.B., Bodin, L., Wulff, C. and Theorell, T., 2015. The relation between office type and workplace conflict: A gender and noise perspective. *Journal of Environmental Psychology*, *42*, pp.161-171.

Davis, M.C., Leach, D.J. and Clegg, C.W., 2011. The physical environment of the office: Contemporary and emerging issues.

De Leeuw, E.D., 2012. Choosing the method of data collection. In International handbook of survey methodology (pp. 113-135). Routledge.

Deloitte., 2022. *Crane Survey Findings.* Available at https://www2.deloitte.com/uk/en/pages/real-estate/articles/crane-survey.html/#/key-findings. [Accessed 19 July 2022].

Department for Education, 2021 Available at https://assets.publishing.service.gov.uk/government/uploads/system/uploads/attachment_data/file/989912/Condition_of_School_Buildings_Survey_CDC1_-_key_findings_report.pdf [Accessed on 22 May 2022].

Di Blasio, S., Shtrepi, L., Puglisi, G.E. and Astolfi, A., 2019. A cross-sectional survey on the impact of irrelevant speech noise on annoyance, mental health and well-being, performance and occupants' behavior in shared and open-plan offices. International journal of environmental research and public health, 16(2), p.280.

Dietrich, P., Eskerod, P., Dalcher, D. and Sandhawalia, B., 2010. The dynamics of collaboration in multipartner projects. Project management journal, 41(4), pp.59-78.

Einola, K. and Alvesson, M., 2021. Behind the numbers: Questioning questionnaires. Journal of Management Inquiry, 30(1), pp.102-114.

Fanning, E., 2005. Formatting a paper-based survey questionnaire: Best practices. Practical Assessment, Research, and Evaluation, 10(1), p.12.

Fielding, M., 2001. Students as radical agents of change. Journal of educational change, 2(2), pp.123-141.

Fleming, J., 2018. Recognizing and Resolving the Challenges of Being an Insider Researcher in Work-Integrated Learning. International Journal of Work-Integrated Learning, 19(3), pp.311-320.

Formica, P., 2016. The 'Coffee Machine Effect'.

Gallo, A., 2014. A refresher on net present value. Harvard Business Review, 19.

Garrett, L.E., Spreitzer, G.M. and Bacevice, P.A., 2017. Co-constructing a sense of community at work: The emergence of community in coworking spaces. Organization studies, 38(6), pp.821-842.

Geldart, P., 2020. The Importance of Seeing the Big Picture. Available at https://www.entrepreneur.com/article/349368 [Accessed on 4th January 2022].

Gov.uk. 2014. *Unprecedented number of new schools opened since 2010*. Available at https://www.gov.uk/government/news/unprecedented-number-of-new-schools-opened-since-2010#:~:text=Since%202010%20the%20government%20has,local%20councils%20or%20Westminster%20politicians. [Accessed 18 July 2022].

Haapakangas, A., Hallman, D.M., Mathiassen, S.E. and Jahncke, H., 2018. Self-rated productivity and employee well-being in activity-based offices: The role of environmental perceptions and workspace use. *Building and Environment*, *145*, pp.115-124.

Haapakangas, A., Hongisto, V., Eerola, M. and Kuusisto, T., 2017. Distraction distance and perceived disturbance by noise—An analysis of 21 open-plan offices. *The Journal of the Acoustical Society of America*, *141*(1), pp.127-136.

Haapakangas, A., Hongisto, V., Varjo, J. and Lahtinen, M., 2018. Benefits of quiet workspaces in open-plan offices–Evidence from two office relocations. *Journal of Environmental Psychology*, *56*, pp.63-75.

Harris, J.L., Sunley, P., Evenhuis, E., Martin, R., Pike, A. and Harris, R., 2020. The Covid-19 crisis and manufacturing: How should national and local industrial strategies respond? Local Economy, 35(4), pp.403-415.

Harris, R., 2015. The changing nature of the workplace and the future of office space. *Journal of Property Investment & Finance*.

Hedge, A., 1982. The open-plan office: A systematic investigation of employee reactions to their work environment. *Environment and Behavior*, *14*(5), pp.519-542.

Hess, J.D. and Benjamin, B.A., 2015. Applying Lean Six Sigma within the university: opportunities for process improvement and cultural change. International Journal of Lean Six Sigma.

Hong, S.M., Godoy-Shimizu, D., Schwartz, Y., Korolija, I., Mavrogianni, A. and Mumovic, D., 2022. Characterising the English school stock using a unified national on-site survey and energy database. Building Services Engineering Research and Technology, 43(1), pp.89-112.

Hongisto, V., Haapakangas, A., Varjo, J., Helenius, R. and Koskela, H., 2016. Refurbishment of an open-plan office–environmental and job satisfaction. *Journal of environmental psychology*, *45*, pp.176-191.

Hox, J.J. and Boeije, H.R., 2005. Data collection, primary versus secondary.

Jahncke, H., Hygge, S., Halin, N., Green, A.M. and Dimberg, K., 2011. Open-plan office noise: Cognitive performance and restoration. Journal of Environmental Psychology, 31(4), pp.373-382.

Johnson, S.M., 2020. Where teachers thrive: Organizing schools for success. Harvard Education Press.

Kane, G.C., Nanda, R., Phillips, A. and Copulsky, J., 2021. Redesigning the post-pandemic workplace. MIT Sloan Management Review, 62(3), pp.12-14.

Kim, J., Candido, C., Thomas, L. and de Dear, R., 2016. Desk ownership in the workplace: The effect of non-territorial working on employee workplace satisfaction, perceived productivity and health. *Building and Environment*, *103*, pp.203-214.

Knight, D.S., Hassairi, N., Candelaria, C.A., Sun, M. and Plecki, M.L., 2022. Prioritizing School Finance Equity during an Economic Downturn: Recommendations for State Policy Makers. Education Finance and Policy, 17(1), pp.188-199.

Kotter, J.P., 2012. Leading change. Harvard business press.

Kotter, J.P., Kotter, J. and Rathgeber, H., 2006. Our iceberg is melting: Changing and succeeding under any conditions. Pan Macmillan.

Kretzmann, M., Shih, W. and Kasari, C., 2015. Improving peer engagement of children with autism on the school playground: A randomized controlled trial. *Behavior Therapy*, *46*(1), pp.20-28.

Larson, M., Cook, C.R., Fiat, A. and Lyon, A.R., 2018. Stressed teachers don't make good implementers: Examining the interplay between stress reduction and intervention fidelity. School Mental Health, 10(1), pp.61-76.

Liu, L., 2016. Using generic inductive approach in qualitative educational research: a case study analysis. Journal of Education and Learning, 5(2), pp.129-135.

Lluent, T., 2022. Befriend Thy Neighbor: Office Seating, Social Networks and Gender. In Academy of Management Proceedings (Vol. 2022, No. 1, p. 11729). Briarcliff Manor, NY 10510: Academy of Management.

Lynch, J. and Wishart, L., 2021. Play diversity and student agency in the redevelopment of a school playspace. *Children's Geographies*, pp.1-15.

Marto, A., Melo, M., Gonçalves, A. and Bessa, M., 2021. Development and evaluation of an outdoor multisensory AR system for cultural heritage. *IEEE Access*, *9*, pp.16419-16434.

Martorell, P., Stange, K. and McFarlin Jr, I., 2016. Investing in schools: capital spending, facility conditions, and student achievement. *Journal of Public Economics, 140*, pp.13-29.

Michigan Tech, Continuous Improvement 2022. Available at https://www.mtu.edu/improvement/learn/what/ [Accessed on 8 July 2022].

Miles, K.H. and Ferris, K., 2015. Designing Schools That Work: Organizing Resources Strategically for Student Success. Education Resource Strategies.

Morin, A.J., Meyer, J.P., Bélanger, É., Boudrias, J.S., Gagné, M. and Parker, P.D., 2016. Longitudinal associations between employees' beliefs about the quality of the change management process, affective commitment to change and psychological empowerment. Human Relations, 69(3), pp.839-867.

Morrison, R.L. and Macky, K.A., 2017. The demands and resources arising from shared office spaces. *Applied ergonomics, 60*, pp.103-115.

Myerson, J. and Ross, P., 2022. Unworking: The Reinvention of the Modern Office. Reaktion Books.

NAHT, 2021. A failure to invest – the state of school funding 2021. Available at https://www.naht.org.uk/News/Latest-comments/News/ArtMID/556/ArticleID/1223/A-failure-to-invest-the-state-of-school-funding-2021 [Accessed on 1 August 2022].

Olsen, C. and St George, D.M.M., 2004. Cross-sectional study design and data analysis. College entrance examination board, 26(03), p.2006.

Olsen, H. and Smith, B., 2017. Sandboxes, loose parts, and playground equipment: a descriptive exploration of outdoor play environments. *Early child development and care, 187*(5-6), pp.1055-1068.

Owens, S., 2021. State of Education Funding (2021). Georgia Budget & Policy Institute https://gbpi. org/state-education-2021.

Pagell, M. and Krause, D.R., 2004. Re-exploring the relationship between flexibility and the external environment. *Journal of Operations Management, 21*(6), pp.629-649.

Paul, S.K. and Chowdhury, P., 2020. A production recovery plan in manufacturing supply chains for a high-demand item during COVID-19. International Journal of Physical Distribution & Logistics Management, 51(2), pp.104-125.

Polley, S., 2013. The Building Regulations 2010. In Understanding the Building Regulations (pp. 15-36). Routledge.

Proctor, K., Adams, R., 2020. *Johnson pledges £1bn school rebuilding programme for England.* Available at https://www.theguardian.com/education/2020/jun/28/johnson-pledges-1bn-over-10-years-for-school-rebuilding-in-england. [Accessed 18 July 2022].

Ramrathan, L., Le Grange, L. and Shawa, L.B., 2017. Ethics in educational research. Education studies for initial teacher education, pp.432-443.

Research Ethics Policy, 2021. University of Buckingham. Available at https://www.bucks.ac.uk/sites/default/files/2021-03/research_ethics_policy.pdf [Accessed on 10 August 2022].

Ryttberg, M. and Geschwind, L., 2017. Professional support staff at higher education institutions in Sweden: Roles and success factors for the job. Tertiary Education and Management, 23(4), pp.334-346.

Sandoval, M. and Messiou, K., 2022. Students as researchers for promoting school improvement and inclusion: a review of studies. International Journal of Inclusive Education, 26(8), pp.780-795.

Saunders, M., Lewis, P. and Thornhill, A., 2003. Research methods forbusiness students. Essex: Prentice Hall: Financial Times.

Saunders, M., Lewis, P.H.I.L.I.P. and Thornhill, A.D.R.I.A.N., 2007. Research methods. Business Students 4th edition Pearson Education Limited, England.

SCHOOL ADMINISTRATORS ARTICLE. Available at https://www.educationworld.com/a_admin/admin/admin540_b.shtml [Accessed 16 July 2022].

Seddigh, A., Berntson, E., Jönsson, F., Danielson, C.B. and Westerlund, H., 2015. The effect of noise absorption variation in open-plan offices: A field study with a cross-over design. Journal of Environmental Psychology, 44, pp.34-44.

Shrestha, P.P. and Zeleke, H., 2018. Effect of change orders on cost and schedule overruns of school building renovation projects. Journal of legal affairs and dispute resolution in engineering and construction, 10(4), p.04518018.

Smite, D., Moe, N.B., Hildrum, J., Huerta, J.G. and Mendez, D., 2022. Work-From-Home is Here to Stay: Call for Flexibility in Post-Pandemic Work Policies. arXiv preprint arXiv:2203.11136.

Sundstrom, E., Town, J.P., Brown, D.W., Forman, A. and Mcgee, C., 1982. Physical enclosure, type of job, and privacy in the office. Environment and Behavior, 14(5), pp.543-559.

Sundstrom, E., Town, J.P., Rice, R.W., Osborn, D.P. and Brill, M., 1994. Office noise, satisfaction, and performance. Environment and behavior, 26(2), pp.195-222.

Tagliaro, C. and Migliore, A., 2021. "Covid-working": what to keep and what to leave? Evidence from an Italian company. Journal of Corporate Real Estate.

Tashakkori, A. and Creswell, J.W., 2007. Exploring the nature of research questions in mixed methods research. Journal of mixed methods research, 1(3), pp.207-211.

Turner, E., 2020. Let's Talk about Flex: Flipping the flexible working narrative for education. John Catt Educational.

Unluer, S., 2012. Being an insider researcher while conducting case study research. Qualitative Report, 17, p.58.

Van Marrewijk, A. and Van den Ende, L., 2018. Changing academic work places: the introduction of open-plan offices in universities. *Journal of Organizational Change Management.*

Veitch, H., 2009. Participation in practice: An evaluation of the primary school council as a participatory tool. Childhoods Today, 21, pp.1-24.

Wang, C.H. and Huang, Y.C., 2000. A new approach to calculating project cost variance. International Journal of Project Management, 18(2), pp.131-138.

Weger, R., Lossio-Ventura, J.A., Rose-McCandlish, M., Shaw, J., Sinclair, S., Pereira, F., Chung, J. and Atlas, L., 2022. "Is there anything else you would like to tell us?": An analysis of language features in text responses to a study on mental health during the COVID-19 pandemic.

Williams, J.J., Hong, S.M., Mumovic, D. and Taylor, I., 2015. Using a unified school database to understand the effect of new school buildings on school performance in England. Intelligent Buildings International, 7(2-3), pp.83-100.

Yılmaz, D. and Kılıçoğlu, G., 2013. Resistance to change and ways of reducing resistance in educational organizations. European journal of research on education, 1(1), pp.14-21.

8 STEPS

THAT WILL MAKE YOU A
SUCCESSFUL & HAPPIER PERSON
IN YOUR SCHOOL.

Often people wonder what the tips and tricks are, to become a successful school leader. Do you know? 8 out of 10 successful people, on average, start from the mindset they have. The success mindset is the initial capital to get a successful life. Not only successful but also a happier person. What are the 8 Steps that successful people in education have in this world that make their lives more comfortable? Everything is wholly and thoroughly discussed in this book.

ABOUT THE AUTHOR

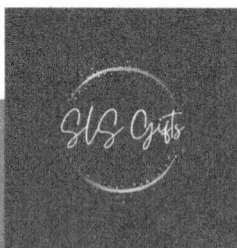

Mr John Evans

The book is written by an experienced school administrator with over 20 years of experience in the field of management and process improvement. The author has a proven track record of improving school administration and has a deep understanding of the challenges and opportunities facing school leaders today.

Printed in Great Britain
by Amazon